BUILD KICKASS TEAMS

LEAD BOLDLY.
HIRE INTENTIONALLY.
FORGE A TEAM THAT ACTUALLY
GIVES A DAMN

PETE SRODOSKI

TABLE OF CONTENTS

Chapter 2: Hiring Kickass People –

Chapter 3: Stage One – Onboard Like a Pro,

INTRODUCTION

If your team doesn't give a damn, that's not their fault. It's yours.

I know that stings to hear, but it's honestly supposed to because the truth is, if you're the one in charge, then every missed deadline, every half-assed effort, and every eye-roll in the conference room is a mirror reflection of your leadership. You can blame the market, point fingers at the talent pool, or shake your head at "kids these days," but at the end of the day, your culture is what you tolerate.

I learned that the hard way. Let me tell you about a time when I was just starting out in my managerial career. There was a time when I hired this guy who seemed very bright on paper, sharp in the interview. First week on the job, though, I catch him in the break room, smearing peanut butter on bread like he's painting the Sistine Chapel. He's taking his time, chatting away, not a care in the world. Meanwhile, the floor is in chaos, customers are stacking up, and deadlines are whistling by like bullet trains. I'm watching him just exist in this little bubble of complacency, and it hit me: *That's on me.*

I hired him and set the expectation. I allowed that level of mediocrity to walk through the door, clock in, and coast, and I knew right then, if I didn't change something, I was going to be the proud owner of a half-baked culture that ran on just enough.

If that's where you are right now, leading a team that's inconsistent, underperforming, or just plain coasting, I get it. You're tired of being the one who always has to step in and clean up the mess. You're tired of carrying that weight, of having to babysit adults who should already know what the hell they're doing. You're scaling and stressed, or maybe you're stuck and settling. Either way, you're on the hook for results, and if you're reading this, it's because you're sick of just surviving.

But here's the thing: This isn't a theory book. This is a no-BS manual for building a team that actually gives a damn. I'm not here to spoon-feed you corporate fluff or 12-step frameworks that sound good on LinkedIn but fall apart in real life. This is the real playbook, the stuff I wish someone had handed me back when I was swimming in excuses and dragging dead weight across the finish line.

WHY I WROTE THIS BOOK

I didn't write this book because I had it all figured out; hell, I wrote it because, at one point, I absolutely didn't. I've hired rock stars and I've hired walking disasters. I've led teams that ran like machines and others that fell apart the second I took a step back. I've made gut-wrenching mistakes, backed the wrong people, avoided the hard conversations I should've had, and paid the price for it.

I've watched good teams rot from the inside because I tolerated B-player behavior. I've seen the wheels come off because I didn't set the standard early enough. I've bitten my tongue when I should've unleashed hell. But I've also seen the other side. I've seen what happens when you get it right. When you build a team that gives a damn. When culture clicks, expectations are crystal clear, and everyone knows they're a part of something worth showing up for.

This book is everything I wish someone had handed me a decade ago. It's not a collection of feel-good theories scribbled on a whiteboard, it's trenches-level leadership. It's the stuff you learn from firing someone who was your top producer but toxic as hell. It's the things you pick up when you turn around a failing department or rebuild a broken team from scratch.

I wrote this for the leaders who are tired of tolerating mediocrity. For the founders scaling fast who need to build a culture that keeps up. For the managers who never got trained but suddenly have people looking to them for answers. And also for the ones who are already damn good but know they can be great.

If you've ever walked into work on a Monday and thought, *Something has to change,* then this book is your blueprint. If you've ever wondered why you're the only one pushing while everyone else just coasts, this is your war map. Also, if you're sick of carrying all the weight yourself, if you're ready to stop being the hero and start building a team that actually carries its own weight, then welcome.

We've got work to do.

WHAT YOU'LL GET

I'm not here to waste your time. This isn't another fluffy leadership book that looks good on your shelf but gathers dust after one skim-through. This is a manual; a dog-eared, coffee-stained, marked-up playbook that you'll drag into Monday meetings and reference before tough conversations.

We're building this around the key pillars of building kickass teams: Leadership, Hiring, Onboarding, Culture, Coaching, Accountability, Conflict, Scaling, Legacy, Habits, and many more. These aren't buzzwords, they're battlegrounds. Each chapter breaks it down, showing you how to actually *win* in these spaces.

Also, I'm not just feeding you theory; at the end of each chapter, you'll get the Monday Morning Playbook. These are real-world action steps that you can put into play immediately. These aren't "think about it" suggestions; these are do-it-now plans, built to move the needle before the coffee even cools.

But that's not all. I'm bringing you inside the real world: proven case studies from the trenches, real-life stories from professionals who built empires from the ground up, and *some* who crashed and burned so you don't have to. We're diving into failed experiences from some of the biggest names in business, the kind of screw-ups that would have sunk lesser leaders, but instead forged them into legends. You're gonna see what happens when things go right... and when they go spectacularly wrong.

Hell, we're even going to take a walk through real-world battles and boardroom brawls, how leaders turned chaos into culture, transformed shaky start-ups into powerhouses, and steered teams through storms that would have sunk lesser ships.

WHAT YOU WON'T GET

Look, if you picked this book up expecting sugar-coated nonsense and corporate cheerleading, put it back. This isn't one of those "Empower Your Synergistic Mindset" bestsellers gathering dust on the airport bookshelf. You're not getting fluff, and you're certainly not getting the same old recycled platitudes wrapped in fancy language.

You also won't find any nine-step frameworks dreamed up by people who've never led a damn thing in their life. No mile-long checklists designed to fill your day with busywork and call it "leadership." I'm not here to fatten up your to-do list, I'm here to cut the fat and get you to the real work of building a team that runs like a warship.

And honestly, you won't get any safe space, everybody-gets-a-trophy BS. Leadership is gritty, it's uncomfortable, and sometimes it's downright brutal. If you want to build a team that can actually go the distance, you're going to have to make the hard calls, fire the wrong people, and raise the bar higher than anyone expects.

What you will get are the raw stories from the field. The ones where things went sideways, where good intentions crashed and burned, and where rebuilding wasn't just necessary, it was nonnegotiable. You'll get the scars and the successes laid out bare, so you can see what it really takes.

This is straight talk for people who actually give a damn. If that's you, turn the page. If not? Well, maybe there's a book about "manifesting leadership vibes" elsewhere.

FINAL RALLY CRY

You don't need permission to lead like this.

You don't even need a title stamped on your door or a board's blessing to build something that matters. You just need the guts to step up, take ownership, and turn that ragtag bunch of average performers into a machine that roars without you.

Honestly, leadership isn't about keeping the lights on, or hitting quotas, or just surviving another quarter. Hell no. It's about building something so solid, so self-sustaining, that when you step back, it *accelerates*. It's about walking away for a week and coming back to find that the ship's running smoother than when you left. It's about creating a team that knows the mission, drives the mission, and defends the mission, whether you're there to crack the whip or not.

When the dust settles, and people look back, they're not going to talk about your PowerPoint skills or how many emails you sent. They're going to talk about what you built. They're going to talk about the team you crafted, how it ran like a warship, how the culture was so damn strong it was unbreakable.

So, I'm asking you right now to make a choice.

Choose to build something that outlasts you, something that doesn't need you to hold its hand. Most importantly, choose to build something that, years from now, people still talk about.

This is it. This is your shot. So, the only question left is… "Are you ready to build something that actually gives a damn?"

No more excuses. No more waiting.

If it's broken, fix it.

If it's messy, lead it.

If it matters, build it.

Let's go.

CHAPTER 1:

OWN THE STANDARD – LEADERSHIP STARTS WITH YOU

I am not afraid of an army of lions led by a sheep; I am afraid of an army of sheep led by a lion.
–Alexander the Great

Your team will never outgrow the strength, clarity, and courage of the one leading it, and that leader is you.

Not your top performer, not your company's values poster, not the morning huddles or motivational speeches; *you*. Great leadership elevates average people. I'm sure we've all observed how weak leadership can sink even the best of them.

Maybe it's a team that used to be a powerhouse. They hit targets, solved problems, moved fast, and had each other's backs. There was momentum and energy. Then slowly, almost without realizing it, something shifted. Deadlines started slipping, communication became unclear, and meetings felt heavier and less focused. The spark was gone, then eventually, you found yourself with a team where everyone was just going through the motions, doing the bare minimum to stay out of trouble. Not because they were lazy or because they didn't care, and certainly not because they didn't believe in the mission, but because leadership failed them. They weren't given clear direction. They didn't know what mattered most anymore, or why. They weren't receiving feedback, so they had no idea if they were doing well or just wasting their time. They weren't challenged to grow or held accountable to a standard. Slowly, they were left to guess about expectations, priorities, and about whether or not their work actually mattered. And here's the thing: When people are left to guess long enough, they stop trying. Not because they don't care, but because they're tired of caring in the dark.

Now, here's what usually happens next: instead of taking ownership, we protect our ego with a neat little phrase: "They just weren't right for the position." However, if we're being honest, they probably *were*. Most people don't show up hoping to fail. They want to contribute, to win, and to be part of something meaningful. They didn't fail the culture— you failed to lead them.

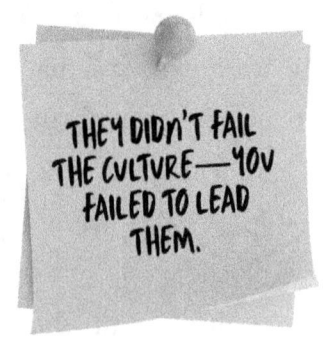

Take, for instance, the Apple story; a fascinating tale of two leaders. In the mid-1980s, Apple was spiraling. Steve Jobs, the passionate visionary who helped start the company, had been ousted. In his place was John Sculley, a seasoned corporate executive from Pepsi. On paper, Sculley had the credentials. However, he lacked one critical quality, which is the ability to lead through uncertainty. Under his leadership, Apple lost its edge, products became dull, innovation stalled, and morale dropped. Sculley focused on management while Apple needed vision. He maintained the status quo when the moment called for bold, uncomfortable moves. Apple began to bleed relevance.

Fast forward to 1997, and Steve Jobs returned. He was the same guy, but this time sharper, more focused, more mature. He cut unnecessary products, clarified Apple's direction, and inspired his team to dream again (Clifford, 2018). He didn't just lead with ideas, he led with conviction, clarity, and decisive action. And the results? Well, the iPod, the iPhone, and the rebirth of Apple into one of the most valuable companies on Earth.

What changed? Not the team or the market—the *leader*. That's the power of leadership. The same people can create radically different results depending on who's leading them. So, understand this: Leadership isn't about charisma or charm. You don't have to be loud, an extrovert, or a "visionary." That stuff might help get attention, but real leadership shows up when things fall apart. When morale dips, when confusion creeps in, and when someone has to stand in the storm and say, "Here's what we do next."

That's why leaders aren't born, they're built. Built through pressure, through repetition, and through the uncomfortable conversations you'd rather avoid. They're shaped by the small, consistent decisions that create culture and drive direction, especially when no one's clapping for you. Leadership is forged in the fire of the toughest moments. When you have to hold someone accountable, even though it might cost you short-term comfort. When you have to make the hard call that no one else wants to own. When every part of you wants to shrink back and keep the peace, but you know silence will cost more in the long run.

That's the job, but unfortunately, this is where leaders often mess up: they think leadership is an achievement, a fancy title, a cute corner office and a lot of respect. Well, it's not, it's a daily responsibility. Once you step into leadership, you don't just own outcomes, you own people—real people, with different personalities, beliefs, backgrounds, and communication styles. And your job? It isn't just to make room for them, it's to create an environment where they can make room for each other even in your absence.

You own their direction, how clearly they understand what matters most, what they're building toward, and why it even matters in the first place. You own their clarity, whether they're guessing or grounded, confused or confident in their role. You own their energy, the way they show up in meetings, how they contribute in presentations, and how motivated they feel to give their best. Also, you own their trust, not just in you, but in the mission, in the team, and in themselves. You're not just about steering the ship, you're stewarding the people on board.

So, when someone starts underperforming, pulling back, or showing signs of disengagement, you don't get to shrug and say, "They're just not motivated." No. You go back to the drawing board and ask:

What changed?

What did they stop hearing?

Is there something I stopped doing?

Remember, leadership means you own the environment, the tone in the room, the clarity of the vision, and the feedback loops or lack of them. You own the culture people are walking into every morning. Most importantly, you don't lead through ego. Also, you don't come in as a savior trying to "fix" everyone. Instead, you lead with clarity, consistency, and courage.

You ask the uncomfortable questions, speak the unspoken and step into the tension, even when it's easier to look away. Essentially, you weren't put here to be liked, you were strategically positioned to lead.

WHAT IS A LEADER?

Before we talk about habits, vision, or even greatness, what does it really mean to be a leader? Strip away the suit, the status, the applause. Forget the corner office, the presidential speech, or the pulpit packed with lights. Leadership has nothing to do with position and everything to do with posture. It is not about titles; it's about a spirit, a presence, a decision to carry something heavier than most are willing to bear—the weight of people, purpose, and the future.

A leader is someone who sees what others don't, steps where others won't, and speaks when others stay silent. They carry vision like a fire in their chest, and they're willing to walk through adversity to protect it. A leader will stand for what they believe in, even if it means standing alone. They don't just want to change situations; they want to transform lives. And they're willing to start with their own. That's the sacred difference. Leaders don't wait for permission, they recognize a calling. They don't need a platform to begin; they build one from nothing if they have to. Some of the world's most powerful leaders started with absolutely no authority, but they had clarity, courage, consistency, and that's often more dangerous than power itself.

Unfortunately, when most people hear the word "leader", they immediately imagine a CEO, a president, or a founder of a company. But there's another figure in the room too; the manager. While both roles are crucial, they are fundamentally different. Where a leader dreams, a manager delivers. Where the leader dares to shake the table, the manager ensures it stands firm. The leader is the architect, designing the blueprint. The manager is the builder, following the plan. One creates the future while the other sustains the now (Greenhalgh, 2023).

To make this difference clearer, picture this:

Aspect	Leader	Manager
Focus	Vision and people	Systems and tasks
Drives	Change and progress	Order and consistency
Power Source	Influence	Authority
Style	Inspires and empowers	Directs and controls
Time Horizon	Long-term impact	Short-term goals
Attitude Toward Risk	Takes bold risks & steps	Avoids uncertainty
Deals With	People, ideas, potential	Plans, performance, processes
Examples	Steve Jobs (innovator)	Tim Cook (operator)

Both roles matter. Every Moses needs an Aaron, and every Jobs needs a Cook, but not everyone is called to be a manager of what is. Some of us are called to be midwives of what will be.

Unfortunately, leadership is not always clean or easy. It's not about applause; it's often about isolation. But truthfully, anyone can become a leader if they're willing to lead themselves first. You don't grow into it by being chosen, you grow into it by *choosing*. Choosing to be disciplined when no one's watching. Choosing to speak up even when your voice shakes. Choosing to carry vision like a secret flame and protect it with everything in you.

So, before you lead teams, families, ministries, or nations, the question is: can you lead yourself? Can you govern your emotions? Your time? Your discipline? Because real leadership doesn't start on the stage, it starts in silence. In the dark when no one's clapping. When no one's calling you "boss." That's where leaders are born. They're not appointed—they're forged.

The world doesn't just need more managers, it needs more leaders. People who are willing to step into chaos with clarity. People who understand that leadership isn't about control, it's about calling. Once you know your calling, no one can manage you back into mediocrity.

THE CORE TRAITS OF A LEADER

However, knowing what a leader is? That's just the beginning. For instance, if leadership is a fire, then character is the wood that keeps it burning. Without the right traits, the title collapses. Furthermore, no one is ever born a leader. Again, you have to become one. Trait by trait, layer by layer. You don't inherit leadership like a trust fund, but you build it like a legacy.

Great leaders, the ones who shift nations, movements, families, and destinies, all carry a collection of core traits that aren't taught in school, but are often forged in adversity. Think of Nelson Mandela, locked in a prison cell for 27 years, yet walking out with dignity and forgiveness instead of vengeance. Or Mother Teresa, who chose the slums over the spotlight. Or Abraham Lincoln, who led a fractured country through civil war, battled depression, and still held firm to moral clarity in the face of chaos.

These traits aren't reserved for the famous or historical, they are the DNA of anyone serious about leading. Whether you're called to lead a nation or just lead your home, the traits are the same. Unfortunately, some of them are painful, but that's the cost we all have to pay to become leaders.

A leader without courage is nothing more than a silent witness. Courage is the backbone of true leadership. If you're afraid of confrontation, afraid of being unpopular, or afraid of standing alone, forget about leading. Leadership requires guts. You must be willing to make the hard decisions when no one else has the spine to step up. Mandela didn't endure his prison stay because it was convenient; he did it because he had a cause greater than himself. If you can't choose what's right over what's easy, leadership will eat you alive.

Vision is what separates true leaders from managers. Anyone can maintain the present, but it takes a visionary to build the future. If you don't see clearly where you're going, don't expect anyone else to follow. People don't follow noise, they follow direction. Steve Jobs envisioned an iPhone when the world was still clinging to buttons. Vision is about foresight, the ability to see what isn't yet visible. Without it, you're just moving people in circles, not forward.

Integrity is the ground you stand on. If your character is shaky, so is your leadership. Leadership is not charisma. It's *consistency*. For instance, Jesus Christ didn't just preach truth, He lived it. And that's what made people follow Him. It wasn't hype, it was authenticity. Leaders with integrity don't lie, don't manipulate, and don't compromise their values for convenience. If people can't trust your heart, they won't trust your direction.

Discipline is also what keeps the machine running when motivation dies. Every great leader operates from discipline, not emotion. They don't wait to feel inspired to act. They act, regardless. Jocko Willink said it best: *Discipline equals freedom* (Willink, n.d.). You can't expect to lead others if you can't lead yourself. Your habits expose you. If you hit snooze more than you hit goals, you've already failed.

Empathy is not weakness; it's wisdom. You can't lead people you don't understand. If you treat people like machines, don't be shocked when they stop moving. Obama connected with people's pain and used it to unite, not manipulate. Empathy builds loyalty, and loyalty is a currency most leaders don't even realize they need. Empathy earns trust, and trust creates movement.

Resilience is the fire test. Adversity doesn't destroy leaders, it reveals them. Leadership is not proven in comfort, it's revealed in chaos. If you fold under pressure, you were never ready to lead in the first place. Churchill held Britain together during one of the darkest chapters in history. Bombs were falling, people were panicking, and still he stood. Real leaders rise in storms, whereas weak ones fumble under pressure. Pain doesn't stop a leader, it trains them.

Humility is what keeps your power in check. Without it, confidence becomes arrogance, and success becomes a ticking time bomb. You're not the hero of the story; the mission is. Angela Merkel, one of the most influential leaders of the 21st century, led Germany and Europe through crisis after crisis, not with flash or ego, but with calm, quiet strength. She rejected lavish praise, avoided the spotlight, and stayed grounded in service. That's humility. It's not about thinking less of yourself; it's about thinking of yourself less. If you can't admit mistakes, seek advice, or learn from others, you've already stopped growing.

Ultimately, servanthood is the true core of leadership. If you think leading means being served, you're already disqualified. Leadership is about lifting others, not elevating yourself. Leadership also isn't about status. It's about sacrifice. You don't lead from a throne, you lead from the ground, with your hands dirty and your heart open.

HABITS

Leadership isn't a title you carry, it's a life you live, and that life is sculpted by the small things you do when no one's watching. It's not your talent that separates you, it's your habits. That's where greatness is born.

A leader's habits are their hidden rituals, the behind-the-scenes grind that produces front-stage impact. You want to see a leader's future? Watch their routines. The way they think. The way they speak. The way they treat people when there's nothing to gain.

I've lived by this one important factor: You don't rise to the level of your goals, you fall to the level of your systems. Discipline is nonnegotiable and every single world-shaker, whether it was Steve Jobs perfecting product design, Jocko Willink training Navy SEALs in extreme ownership, or Kobe Bryant taking 800 jump shots before dawn, they had patterns that birthed power.

If your habits are weak, your leadership will always crack under pressure. You don't need more hype, you need better rhythms. Strategic, intentional, daily practices that build focus, resilience, vision, and execution. This is how leaders are forged.

Now, let's break down the core habits that separate the average from the impactful, the ones that turn potential into legacy.

Early Rising

Discipline starts at dawn. Great leaders don't sleep in on purpose. They own their mornings. Why? Because the early hours are when distractions are silent and the mind is sharp. Whether it's journaling, praying, planning, reading, or training, the first few hours set the tone for the rest. You don't control your day unless you command your morning. A good example is Apple's Tim Cook who wakes up at 3:45 a.m. to get ahead of the day because pressure respects preparation.

Cut the Crap - Ruthless Prioritization

If everything matters, nothing matters. Leaders know what's urgent, what's important, and what's noise. They don't drown in to-do lists. They identify the vital few and eliminate the trivial many. Focus is a weapon, and busyness is a trap. Without clarity, your energy gets hijacked.

Relentless Self-Education

Leaders read. Leaders learn. They don't wait for a classroom or a course. They seek wisdom, mentors, books, podcasts, interviews—anything that expands their mind, really. They know that what they feed their mind shapes their vision and their decisions. For instance, Elon Musk learned rocket science by reading and asking questions. No degree. Just hunger.

Emotional Mastery

You don't get to be unstable and still lead well. You'll face critics, betrayal, pressure, and chaos. However, if you can't master your emotions, your emotions will master your leadership. Leaders feel, but they don't get led by feelings. They process, pause, and respond—they don't react.

Integrity in the Shadows

Who you are in secret is who you really are. Leadership isn't just a performance, it's a reflection. What you do when no one's watching will eventually show up when everyone is. Cut corners privately, lose credibility publicly. Habits of honesty, restraint, and accountability are the foundation of unshakable influence. When no one would've noticed, Abraham Lincoln once walked miles to return a few cents from an overcharge at his store. That kind of integrity doesn't go unnoticed.

Obsess Over Feedback – It's Your Superpower

You grow by knowing what's broken. Real leaders aren't defensive, and they certainly don't crumble under critique. They invite it, study it, and evolve. They ask hard questions like, "Where am I falling short?", "What did I miss?", and "How can I get better?" Feedback is a growth mirror, and most people avoid it. Leaders, though? They crave it.

Health as a Priority

You can't pour from an empty cup, and no, coffee doesn't count. Burned-out leaders don't make brave decisions; they make dumb ones. If your body's crashing, your mind's next. Leadership is a long-haul flight, not a TikTok sprint. You need stamina. That means eating like a grown-up, moving like you've got knees that work, and sleeping like your destiny depends on it, because it kind of does.

So, put on those crusty running shoes and take a jog in the morning. Not for the "aesthetic," but for survival. Your vision needs oxygen.

Why It All Matters

Now, you may be wondering if all this was necessary or if it's just fluff. Well, knowing the traits and habits of leadership is very much necessary for transformation. If you don't understand the internal engine that drives leaders, you'll fumble the wheel when it's your turn to drive. Every habit you adopt shapes how you carry the weight of leadership. You don't build winning teams with weak foundations. You don't command respect if you can't first command yourself.

Discipline, integrity, and vision are tools that you'll need when things get tough, when people are watching or not, and when decisions hang in the balance. If you skip this part, you'll regret it when the pressure hits. This is the groundwork. Everything else you build will stand or fall on it.

THE COST OF ADMISSION: WHAT LEADERSHIP REALLY DEMANDS

So by now, you should know that leadership is not a throne, it's a toll gate. You don't get the role without paying the price. Unfortunately, the price isn't your charm, your IQ, or how loud your voice is in a meeting. It's discipline. It's backbone. It's the ability to hold a standard even when it's unpopular or inconvenient. The truth is, leadership is less about control and more about consistency. If your people can't trust your character, they won't trust your direction, no matter how impressive your resume looks.

Everything you believe, feel, or notice about your team? You owe it to them to say it. Keeping quiet isn't mercy, it's sabotage. You're not helping anyone by watching them drown in silence. Real leaders don't gossip in corners; they confront in truth. If someone on your team is off course, it's your duty to speak. That's the job. That's the weight of the role. You don't get to look the other way and still call yourself a leader.

Fairness, transparency, and consistency are the cost of admission. You don't earn respect for having them, you disqualify yourself if you don't. People don't need a boss who plays favorites. They need someone who makes decisions from a clear center.

Someone whose actions don't change depending on who's in the room or how the wind blows because if your leadership isn't stable, your team won't be either.

Now, let me pause right here and give you something worth journaling, maybe even printing, framing, and hanging where you can see it every day: You don't ever need to apologize for holding the line. Expecting people to show up on time, to respect others, to do what they say they're going to do, that's not being "hard." That's called being serious about excellence. These aren't outrageous demands, these are the bare minimum, and everyone in your team should learn it, live it, and love it.

I've had to learn this the hard way, feeling like I was asking for too much, second-guessing myself for expecting discipline, feeling guilty for calling things out. Well, the truth is, when you lower the bar to accommodate people who don't want to grow, you're not being kind, you're being careless and that can and will only harm your vision.

Leadership isn't about dragging people who refuse to move. It's about walking with those who are willing to grow and giving them the recognition they deserve, too. Sometimes, the best thing you can do for someone is not to rescue them, but to challenge them. Hold the line and set the standard. Let the bar stay high, and the ones who are ready will rise, whereas the ones who aren't? Well, that's not on you.

So, as a leader, you're always on display. Your silence might be mistaken for consent, which gives permission. Your sloppiness gives license. If you let it slide once, they'll assume it doesn't matter. But if you stand your ground, people will rise to meet you.

Forget the speeches and motivational quotes. Your actions are signals, and every single day, you're sending one through your habits, reactions, and standards. So no, this isn't the feel-good part of leadership, but it is the real part that very few will tell you about, and if you can't pay the cost, don't expect the title to mean anything.

SET THE STANDARD, DON'T JUST TALK IT

At this point, you know what's required of you. You've sharpened your habits, and you've understood the cost and owned the title. Now, it's time to make sure everyone else around you knows what game we're playing and what it takes to win.

Cristiano Ronaldo is one of the most celebrated soccer players in the world. Trophies, records, awards, you name it. And he's not just a player, he's an entire brand of dominance. What people often miss about him, though, is that his greatness isn't just raw talent—it's a lifestyle. The man trains harder than most rookies. He's the first on the pitch and the last to leave. This is not something for show; it's a signal, a standard.

Ronaldo doesn't beg his teammates to step up—he demands it. Not because he's arrogant, but because he lives the expectation himself. There's a story about how he once stormed the locker room after a weak performance from the team, furious not because they lost, but because the fight wasn't there. Most people view that as drama, but I actually see it as leadership. He sets the tone in the gym, in practice, on the field, and in the culture because if you're on his team, the bar is excellence.

You don't get excellence by hoping for it. You get it by defining it early, clearly, and unapologetically. What you allow is what will continue, and what you ignore becomes invisible permission (Murillo, 2017). So, if you want your team to rise, the altitude has to be set from the Genesis. Just like Ronaldo's team knows what kind of intensity he expects, your people need to know what kind of leader you are and what kind of culture you're cultivating.

So, what does that look like in different setups and environments? Let's look at a few examples:

If you're leading a team in a corporate setting, clear expectations might look like this:

- Everyone checks in by 9 a.m. without excuses.
- Weekly deliverables are due every Friday by 3 p.m. Period.
- If you say you're going to do something, it gets done.

If you're a coach or creative lead:

- We don't skip rehearsals, even if we're tired.
- You're expected to review your material before team sessions.
- Excellence isn't something we hope for; it's what we train for.

If you're in a more flexible or start up environment:

- Communication is key—ghosting is not tolerated.
- We respect deadlines because we respect each other's time.
- "That's not my job" isn't in our vocabulary.

If you're in a school environment (principal, department head, or class leader):

- Every assignment must be submitted on time—extensions aren't the norm.
- If you're late to class, you're interrupting the learning. We don't normalize it.

- Respect for classmates and staff isn't optional—it's part of showing up.

In a church leadership setting (youth leader, worship team, elders):

- If you're on the schedule, you show up early, not just on time.
- We rehearse before we lead worship. We don't "wing it" and call it spiritual.
- When we commit to something in ministry, we treat it with the same honor as any job.
- Gossip doesn't fly here. We build people up, we don't tear them down.

Volunteering or NGO team:

- Volunteering is a commitment, not a backup plan for when you're free.
- Everyone pulls their weight; unpaid doesn't mean unaccountable.
- We respond to messages promptly. People's lives may depend on what we do.

In a remote or freelance team:

- Updates are part of the job. If you're working, we shouldn't have to guess it.
- If you're blocked or delayed, you speak up. Silence is not a strategy.
- Flexibility isn't a loophole for sloppiness. Deliver what you promised, when you promised it.

No matter the context—corporate, creative, church, or classroom—the same rule applies: unclear expectations breed unmet standards. Those unmet standards will, in turn, quietly rot your culture from the inside out. Think of it like taking a number at the deli. You might have to wait a while, but because you know where you stand, you don't get frustrated. You understood what you were signing up for, and you agreed to the terms upfront. That's what clear expectations do: they eliminate confusion and give people the dignity of direction. So, don't wait until after a mistake to set the rules because by then, it's already too late. You'll find yourself with a team full of talent but lacking clarity, just like Chelsea FC in the 23/24 season.

See, they were up 4–0 against Everton, cruising. A penalty gets awarded, and instead of a celebration, chaos breaks out. Cole Palmer, who was already on a hat-trick and the designated penalty taker, stepped up, but then so did Jackson and Madueke. Suddenly, it's not soccer, it's an episode of *Survivor* – alliances, ego, and public chaos. Three players squabbling over one penalty. The captain had to break it up, and the coach was visibly furious while all of it played out on live TV.

That's what happens when you have expectations without clarity. When roles aren't defined, confusion is inevitable, and with it, public embarrassment, broken trust, and a fraying team chemistry.

So, take this seriously: set expectations before the game begins. Make the rules clear from day one. When standards are obvious, culture becomes stable, and when culture is strong, results are almost guaranteed. I say "almost" because there's one more ingredient that separates a solid culture from a truly elite one, and that's clarity around excellence.

You can have all the rules in place. You can have a team that shows up, that's committed, that follows instructions. However, without a shared understanding of what good actually looks like and what "done well" truly means, your team might still fall short. They're playing the game, yes, but without a clear scoreboard and fixed goalposts.

BLUEPRINTS OF EXCELLENCE

In leadership, setting expectations is crucial, but on its own, it's not enough. Why? Because even if the rules are clear, people still need to know what great looks like. Otherwise, they'll aim for the bare minimum, and this isn't because they're lazy, but because no one ever showed them how far they could go. That's where you come in, not just as the one who sets the standard, but the one who embodies it.

There's one man who inspired me deeply, even to this day, and his name is Major Richard Winters. He wasn't your typical celebrity general. He didn't chase the spotlight or throw around his rank, but when everything around him was unstable, from the chaotic drop into Normandy on D-Day to the freezing trenches of Bastogne, Winters was anchored, calm, clear, and disciplined to say the least (Archives, 2023). He led not with noise, but with presence, and he was the kind of leader who made others want to rise, not because he demanded it, but because he demonstrated it. He didn't give speeches, he gave direction, and he'd always lead from the front.

One of his most famous moves—the assault on a heavily fortified German artillery position with only a small unit—is still studied at West Point today. This is because it wasn't just a win, it was a masterclass in tactical excellence, resourcefulness, and steady courage. Winters didn't move the goalposts, he defined them, made them visible, and then walked toward them with unwavering resolve.

That's what excellence looks like in action, and that's your job, too. When you don't define what good looks like, you leave your team in the dark, and that's how mediocrity takes root. However, when excellence is visible and consistent, it becomes contagious. People calibrate themselves to what they see, not just what they're told. So, what does this look like outside of a battlefield?

Let's bring it closer to home:

- In a corporate setting, maybe "good" looks like showing up early to meetings, delivering results without excuses, and responding to emails within 24 hours. Not because you're a robot but because your actions set the pace. If your team sees you respecting timelines, they'll mirror that rhythm.

- In a creative environment, "good" might be staying open to feedback, pushing the boundaries of an idea, and showing up to rehearsals even when inspiration feels flat. The leader who prepares thoroughly, honors the process, and still fights for beauty even when no one's watching, because that's who defines the bar.

- In a classroom or educational setting, it could look like always being prepared, treating students with respect, and holding consistent discipline. Not because it's easy, but because it creates safety, focus, and growth.

- In a start-up space, where things move fast and roles shift quickly, "good" might be overcommunicating, owning mistakes, and maintaining momentum through chaos. A leader who remains steady in uncertainty gives the team a benchmark of excellence to aim for, not perfection, but progress with integrity.

There are many examples we can consider, but nevertheless, if you, as the leader, never pause to breathe, reflect, or replenish, you'll burn out, and trust me, burnout kills excellence. A leader who runs on fumes teaches their team that exhaustion is a virtue when it's not. Margin is, rest is, and boundaries are. You're not doing your people any favors by being a martyr. Model balance, clarity, and model presence, the kind that says, "I care enough to show up fully, and I expect the same from you."

Honestly, when your team knows what "good" looks like, not as a moving target, but as a shared, lived standard, they start chasing it without being pushed. Excellence becomes the rhythm, not the rule. And the beauty of this is that when your culture gets to that point, you don't have to constantly correct, you lead less with force and more with gravity. Your example begins to lead for you. So yes, set expectations, but then go one step further: embody them. If you don't, guaranteed someone else will define "good" for your team, and it probably won't be good at all. And this brings us to one of the most overlooked, dangerous costs in leadership.

COST OF POOR LEADERSHIP

You can build expectations or even model them, but if the culture underneath isn't protected, if it's not reinforced with consistency and courage, and cracks start forming. Quiet at first, then louder, right up until the entire foundation shifts.

I've come to learn an uncomfortable truth, one that many aren't ready to accept because it cuts a little too deep: people don't always quit jobs; they quit leadership. And when they do, it's rarely loud. They don't slam doors or send dramatic goodbye emails. They just begin to fade. The passion dims. The questions stop. Ideas dry up. And slowly, without ever saying it outright, they stop showing up with their full self.

That's the quiet exit, the kind that does the most damage. Not because someone left the building, but because they stayed… and checked out anyway. That's the real cost, not in salaries, but in silent exits.

It's like watching the 2022 Denver Broncos — stacked with talent, a high-profile quarterback in Russell Wilson, and huge expectations. But behind the scenes? Misalignment. Coaching confusion. Locker room disconnect. On paper, they looked like contenders. On the field, they were a mess.

No one trusted the system, and without trust in leadership, the game was already lost before kickoff. Excellence in public can't mask chaos in private for long.

When leadership lacks clarity or conviction, dysfunction fills the gap. Toxicity doesn't show up overnight, it creeps in through side comments, blame games, missed deadlines, and the slow erosion of accountability. It's not explosive; it's corrosive, and it eats everything, starting with belief, then ownership, and then results.

People stop fighting when they feel like leadership has stopped caring. They stop trying to build when they feel like no one's really guarding what's being built. They stop dreaming when no one dares to define what winning actually looks like.

Culture doesn't collapse in a single moment. It dies quietly. In meetings that feel pointless. In silences that go unaddressed. In standards that slip, and leaders who flinch when it's time to reinforce them.

So, if you've been wondering why the energy in your team feels off or perhaps your best people aren't showing up like they used to, and the fire that once fueled your vision now flickers faintly, it might not be the people; it might be the leadership.

That's the cost of neglect. The price of soft silence in the face of slipping standards. Clarity is what builds culture, confusion is what tears it down. Once decay sets in, it spreads faster than most leaders realize, infecting morale, trust, and performance in a matter of weeks if not days.

This is your chance to stop that before it starts. Or to reverse it before it's too late.

LEAD WITH CLARITY

Leadership isn't just about setting the bar, it's about showing people what reaching it looks like. That's the thread we've been pulling throughout this journey so far. However, to really drive it home, let me give you something deceptively simple. A few years ago, I heard this analogy at a leadership seminar in Michigan. It was framed as a joke at first, but it stuck with me ever since:

If you ask eight people to make a peanut butter and jelly sandwich, you'll get eight different sandwiches. One person uses crunchy peanut butter, another floods the bread with jelly. Some cut diagonally, some don't cut at all. White bread, brown bread, sourdough, neat, messy, light-handed, and heavy-handed—you name it.

However, every single one of them will tell you confidently, "I did what you asked."

Now, were they wrong? Technically, no. But were they aligned? Absolutely not.

That's exactly what happens when you don't define what good looks like. You'll get effort, action, but you won't get consistency. You also won't get excellence, and the most dangerous part is that you'll think the problem is your people when the real issue is your clarity. So, whether it's how to run a meeting, manage a client call, or handle conflict, don't just tell people what to do. Show them how to win because if they fail while guessing, you didn't lead them, you left them guessing, and that's how you ended up with eight different sandwiches and zero alignment.

So, what do we do with all this? How do we take all these ideas and make them real, starting now, not someday? That's what the Monday Morning Playbook is for.

MONDAY MORNING
PLAYBOOK

Leadership is an obligation. Your team deserves clarity, direction, and truth, even when it's uncomfortable. If something is stuck in your head that affects their growth, it needs to get out. That's your job.

🧠 MINDSET SHIFT:

Leadership isn't something you turn on and off when it's convenient. Growth happens.

✓ DO THIS MONDAY:

1. Pick One Team Member You've Been Holding Back Feedback From (By End of Day Today)

- You already know who it is, the person you've been tiptoeing around because the conversation is uncomfortable.
- Write down what's in your head. Be specific. If you were in their shoes, would you want to know this?
- If the answer is yes, schedule the conversation today. Not tomorrow. Today.
- Say this: "I want to be clear with you because I care about your growth. Here's what I've noticed, and here's what I think we need to do about it."

2. Write Out "What Good Looks Like" for One Repeating Task (By This Week)

- Use the PB&J Test: If five people did this task, would it look five different ways? If yes, you haven't defined it clearly enough.
- Write it out:
  - What's the outcome?
  - What are the expectations?
  - What does "great" look like?
- Share it with the team or the individual who owns that task. If they don't know the standard, they can't hit it.

3. Audit Your Non-negotiables (Today)

- List out the "cost of admission" expectations on your team:
  - Showing up on time.
  - Following through on promises.
  - Owning mistakes without excuses.
- **Ask yourself:** Am I holding everyone to this? If not, why not?
- If you're letting anyone slide, you're lowering the standard. Fix it before it spreads.

CHAPTER 2:

HIRING KICKASS PEOPLE – FINDING ASSETS, AVOIDING LIABILITIES

"If you think it's expensive to hire a professional, wait until you hire an amateur."
– Red Adair

There's a moment in business history that teaches more about leadership failure than most business books ever will. In 2001, Enron was riding high; a global powerhouse with billions in revenue and a reputation for innovation. But beneath the surface, corruption was festering. Executives gamed the system, manipulated financial statements, and built their empire on lies. When the collapse came, it didn't just wipe out a company; it obliterated $74 billion in shareholder value, destroyed countless careers, and shattered public trust (Bondarenko, 2025b).

That's the power of one wrong person—or a handful of them. It doesn't matter how elite your team is. You can have brilliance in every chair, excellence in every department, but if you've got even a single leader poisoning the well, it's only a matter of time before the whole organism shuts down.

Leadership isn't just about building great teams, it's about defending them. It's about protecting the culture you bled for and guarding the mission from anything or anyone that threatens to rot it from the inside out. That, however, means making the hard call.

Not every underperformer is a lost cause, though. Some people are discouraged, disoriented, or simply disconnected. They don't need to be fired, they need to be led. A good coach can reignite someone like that. With vision, clarity, and value, they bounce back stronger. But then some aren't just underperforming, they're undermining, whispering doubt, dodging responsibility, and resisting correction. These are slow leaks that you keep patching until the entire crew drowns. Wise leaders learn the difference.

They understand that waiting for things to magically improve isn't kindness, it's negligence. That "just one more chance" can cost the entire team their morale. Energy spreads and culture echoes. One unchecked corner-cutter, one passive-aggressive saboteur, and suddenly your high-performers are questioning why they show up early, why they give their best, why they bother.

You can't build a championship team while babysitting toxicity. Unfortunately, this is what most people miss: that those people don't just show up by accident. You attract them when you're unclear. You keep them when your standards are flexible, and you tolerate them when your leadership gets soft. That's why hiring isn't just a decision, it's a battlefield move. It's war strategy, strategic alignment, and culture defense. It's about guarding the gates and elevating the standard so high that only the right ones make it through because the wrong person won't just slow you down, they'll rob you of momentum. They'll erode morale, twist values, and leave damage that high-performing teams take months, sometimes years, to bounce back from.

Some people carry weight, others add weight, but the weight you tolerate becomes the standard your team lives under. So, the mission is simple: find assets and filter out liabilities. Build teams that don't just function, they fly. This is how you protect what you've built and scale what you believe in—one intentional hire at a time.

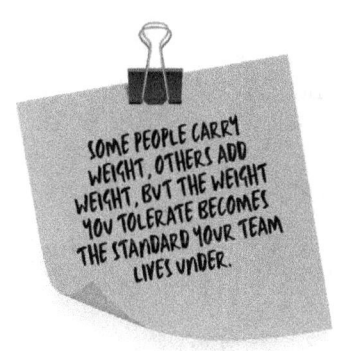

SOME PEOPLE CARRY WEIGHT, OTHERS ADD WEIGHT, BUT THE WEIGHT YOU TOLERATE BECOMES THE STANDARD YOUR TEAM LIVES UNDER.

START HIRING, EVEN WHEN YOU'RE NOT

One of the deadliest mistakes a leader can make is waiting until they're desperate to start hiring. When you're in urgent need, your standards drop, and you stop thinking strategically. You stop asking, "Does this person fit our culture?" and start asking, "Can they start Monday?", and the moment you settle, you start bleeding culture. You compromise the very thing you worked so hard to build. The sharpest leaders know better. They understand that hiring isn't an event, it's a posture. You're not just hiring to plug a hole, you're scouting for future allies before the battle begins. That means staying in recruitment mode even when your organization chart looks "full."

Having a full team is not enough. You need a ready bench as well because, honestly, the hiring process takes time. When you finally post a role, you've got a narrow window, maybe two solid weeks before the best candidates get snatched by someone else. And if you're only starting your search, then you're already behind. You'll end up choosing from what's available, not from what's ideal.

Take sports, for instance. In every elite team, there's a backup for every position. You think the coach only starts scouting when a player gets injured? No. There's already someone warming up, trained, aligned, and ready to go. They've been watching from the sidelines, soaking in the playbook, and waiting for their number to be called. This is because in high-stakes environments, there's no time to panic-hire.

Imagine a basketball team losing their point guard and tossing the waterboy into the game. That's what happens in business when you hire out of desperation: you end up with someone completely unfit running plays they don't understand. Now your team's confused, your pace slows down, and you start losing momentum.

Also, it's not just sports. In warfare, you never send your best generals to the front line without a contingency plan. Commanders keep reserves. There are layers of leadership, specialized units, and backup logistics in place long before a bullet is fired. Why? Because battles are unpredictable, and losing one leader, one critical piece, can throw the whole mission off balance. Now, imagine going to war with one archer, no quiver, and a slingshot from aisle five of a toy store. That's what happens when you don't plan for depth. You risk everything on one person, hoping they don't break, burn out, or bail.

Hiring should never be reactive. Because when you're backed into a corner, your emotions start doing the interviews, and emotions don't care about red flags; they care about relief. That's how liabilities sneak in, and that's how you end up with a former accountant running your sales department because "he's got people skills." That's how your culture starts to wobble: slowly, then suddenly. You wouldn't hire a goalie to play offense, would you? So, stop dragging whoever's available into roles they're not designed for just because you're under pressure. It's not fair to them, and it's deadly for the mission. Smart leaders don't wait for roles to open, they keep the hiring pipeline warm. They build relationships with talented people before they're needed. They stay connected to industry circles. They mentor, scout, and invest in their future team in advance because when the moment comes and it always comes they don't scramble. They select.

Hire for Alignment, Not Impressions

Smart leaders don't just wing it when it's time to hire. They define what winning actually looks like before they shake a single hand or post a single job. Because when you're vague about what you're looking for, you'll end up with people who are vague about how they show up. This is where role scorecards come in, not as some corporate HR gimmick, but as a strategic filter that protects your standards and ensures you're not just hiring for talent, but for alignment.

A role scorecard isn't a job description, it's a blueprint for success. It doesn't just list what the person will do, it defines what a win looks like in that seat. It outlines the mission of the role, the key outcomes expected, the cultural traits required, and how performance will actually be measured. One trap most leaders fall into is posting job ads filled with vague buzzwords, "team player," "self-starter," "good communication skills," but those don't mean the same thing to everyone. What you're imagining when you say "team player" might be someone who proactively supports their teammates, but what they're hearing could just mean someone who doesn't start fights in the group chat.

Without clarity, there's no alignment, and without alignment, you're not hiring an asset; you're flipping a coin. So, before you open that door to applicants, sit down and define it:

- What does this role really exist to do?
- What are the top three outcomes they must drive in the next 6–12 months?
- What kind of thinking, behavior, and energy are required to thrive in this seat?
- What non-negotiables can't be taught and therefore must be found?

Don't just define the *what*, define the *how*. It's not just that they hit targets, it's how they hit them. Did they bulldoze people to get there, or did they elevate the room while doing it? Remember, your brand isn't built by outcomes alone, it's shaped by the energy that creates those outcomes. This is why hiring can't just be about the resume. Resumes tell you what someone has done, but a great role scorecard tells you whether what they've done is what you actually need. It's the lens you'll use to assess fit, not just qualifications, because sometimes the most qualified person is also the least aligned, and while they may look like a gift on paper, they'll unravel your culture faster than you can say, "Maybe we should've asked more questions."

The clarity you bring into the hiring process will either sharpen your selection or blind it. When you're clear, you don't just filter better, you attract better. Your job posts speak differently, your interviews cut deeper, and your confidence to say "no" to the wrong person skyrockets.

So no, this isn't about hiring the most impressive person, it's about hiring the most aligned person. The one who doesn't just match your mission but strengthens it. You don't get there by guessing, you get there by being painfully clear about what you need, what you can't compromise on, and what winning in your world actually looks like.

Apply Pressure

Once you've got your role scorecard dialed in, and when you know the mission, the expectations, and what winning looks like, it's time to filter. And you're not filtering just for skill but for alignment. Why? Because trust me, there's ChatGPT nowadays, and as such, resumes are a trap. Portfolios can be polished, and even interviews can lie. However, things like character, patterns, and values don't hide for long if you know where to look. Filtering isn't just about asking better questions, it involves building a process that reveals who someone truly is when the lights are off, when pressure hits, or when nobody's watching. Take it as though you're not hiring for performance in peace, you're hiring for resilience in war.

Now, one of the most powerful ways to filter is by engineering your process to expose patterns. Think of every stage as a doorway, and with each doorway, you're watching how they walk through it. Are they on time? Do they follow instructions? How do they respond to feedback? Do they communicate like a teammate or a solo artist? You're not just evaluating their *what*, you're reading their *how*.

Let's say your team values ownership. Then don't just ask, "Do you consider yourself someone who takes ownership?" Anyone can say yes. Instead, watch how they behave across the entire process. Did they send a follow-up? Did they take the initiative to research the company? Did they prepare thoughtful questions? Those micro-decisions are loud. They tell you everything. Remember that people don't rise to the level of your values; they fall to the level of their habits. With that in mind, the real filtering happens when you create enough friction in your process that people either rise through it or quietly disqualify themselves.

Do you want people who are proactive? Add a step where they have to solve a small problem. Perhaps you want people who care about communication? Watch how they respond to vague instructions. How about people who value feedback? Give them some and see what they do with it. This doesn't mean making the process unnecessarily long or robotic; it means making it intentional. It means making it purpose-built to catch the details that reveal someone's DNA. One thing's for sure, you can train someone's skills, but you can't install their values. So, build your hiring process like you're building a filter for the soul. That's what great teams are made of. Some of the best leaders in the world don't just hire, they design filters so strong, the wrong people never even make it through the front door.

Take Netflix, for example: their culture deck went viral not just because of how bold it was but because of how brutally honest it was. It didn't sugarcoat the expectations, didn't coddle, and also made it crystal clear: if you're not high-performing, self-managing, and mature enough to handle radical candor, this isn't your place (McCord, 2014). That deck was the filter. Before you even stepped into the interview, the values either drew you in or weeded you out. And that's the point: great culture doesn't just attract, it repels.

Now, zoom out to the military world. Navy SEALs have arguably one of the most grueling selection processes on Earth. But here's what's wild: it's not just about physical toughness. It's psychological. It's emotional. It's spiritual. Why? Because in war, skill without grit is dangerous. Talent without mental endurance gets people killed. That's why their entire pipeline is a filter designed to push you to the edge—not to break you, but to reveal you. The point isn't to make it hard for the sake of it, the point is to expose who you really are when comfort is gone. Now, let's bring that back to business. See, you're not running boot camp, but you are building a culture, so be intentional and unapologetic.

PRESSURE-TEST THE INTERVIEW

This is the moment where most leaders either get sharpened or scammed. A lot of people show up to interviews with rehearsed charm, buzzwords, and just enough polish to make you think they're gold. However, charisma isn't character, and confidence isn't competence.

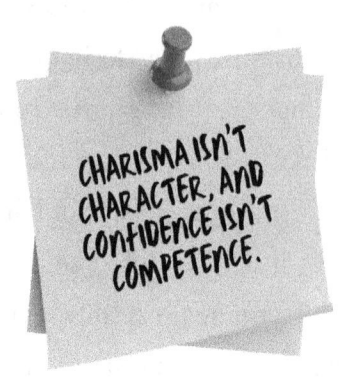

The best leaders know the difference. They're not hiring based on vibes, they're filtering for values. Why's that? Because at this stage, you're not just trying to see who can do the job, you're trying to find out who will do the job the way it needs to be done according to your standards.

This is why the best interviews aren't about Q&A, they're about X-ray. You're looking past the answers into the patterns. You want stories, not scripts. You're listening for how they think, how they take ownership, how they respond when things go sideways. Anybody can talk a big game but how do they act under pressure? When they failed, did they blame others or take responsibility? When they had a conflict, did they seek resolution or burn bridges?

Let them speak, but lead the conversation. Ask them about the last time they got negative feedback. Watch how they respond. Do they flinch? Do they get defensive? Or do they own it and explain how they adapted? Ask them about a team experience that didn't go well. See if they throw their coworkers under the bus or if they reflect on their own part in the breakdown. What you're looking for isn't perfection, it's self-awareness.

Let me give you a secret sauce I've gathered over the years: don't just ask them what they've done, ask them what they've *learned*. Execution is one thing, but evolution is another. A person who can evolve, reflect, and level up after a hit? That's someone worth betting on. You're not hiring artificial intelligence or robots, you're building a team of thinkers, owners, problem-solvers. So, your questions have to go deeper than, "Tell me about a time when…" and move toward, "What did that moment teach you and how are you different because of it?"

Also, be wary of people who overpromise. If someone says "Yes" to everything, dig a little deeper. Strong candidates will also tell you what they *can't* do, where they're still growing, or what they're currently learning. That honesty is gold, and that's the transparency you should be targeting. It shows that they know themselves, and it demonstrates that they're not just trying to impress, they're trying to align. You're not casting the next star of *Mission: Impossible*—you're building a team that can show up, day in and day out, when the cameras are off. In the real world, consistency and character always beat charisma.

Another key move is to watch their energy—not just what they say, but how they say it. Are they asking questions, too, or just trying to survive the conversation? Normally, the best hires come in curious. They want to understand the mission. They want clarity on expectations, and that's a good sign. People who are serious about contribution don't just want a seat, they want to know the direction the ship is sailing.

At the end of the day, you're not the only one asking questions, they're interviewing you, too. That dynamic matters from the very first word. The whole purpose of this process goes beyond putting on a show, it's about discovering if there's a match worth building something real with. So, don't rush it, don't fake it, and don't overtalk to fill silence. Let the conversation breathe. The right people will show up with truth, not theatrics. If you're really doing it right, the best ones won't just walk away excited, they'll leave feeling challenged as though they were seen, stretched, and respected. That's how you know the interview did its job.

HIRE LIKE IT'S YOUR LEGACY ON THE LINE

I once heard a story about a start-up founder who hired his best friend as Head of Sales. They'd grown up together, shared dorm rooms, vacations, and even godfathered each other's kids. It felt like the most natural hire in the world. Six months in, though, revenue was flatlining. The team was frustrated. Deadlines were missed. Accountability was nowhere, and when the founder tried to call him out, the response was, "Bro, respectfully, we've been through too much for you to talk to me like that, please put some respect on me and lower your tone."

Boom, game over. That company never recovered. This is the moment where leadership gets tested. Not in the boardroom, not in the vision-casting sessions, but in the quiet, uncomfortable decisions about who you let through the gates and, more importantly, why you let them in.

That's why we're not just talking about resumes and reference calls, we're talking about warfare. We're talking about defending your culture like it's a castle. Why? Because one wrong hire can let in termites that quietly eat everything from the inside out.

So, now that you've learned how to interview with purpose, how to listen for alignment, how to ask deeper questions, and how to treat interviews like a mission briefing rather than a charm contest, you need to zoom in on the battleground where the real damage happens—and that's not during the interview, it's all in the decision-making that comes after.

It's time to talk about the dangerous hires, the convenient hires, the sentimental hires, and the kind that feel right in the moment but cost you everything long-term.

You can almost hear the celebration music when a founder makes their first big hire. Cue the champagne, cue the LinkedIn announcement, cue the "We're so excited to welcome…"

Now pause because this right here is where the right hire can build an empire, or the wrong hire can burn it to the ground, and more often than not, the worst hire is the easiest one. That's the part nobody warns you about. It's the cousin who's "in between jobs," the friend who's always been there, the guy who knows a little about marketing because he once boosted a Facebook post for his mom's candle business. Convenience is a trap, and when you hire from a place of comfort, sentiment, or desperation, you're guaranteed to pay for it with interest.

This is where leaders stand out. This is because leadership isn't just about setting vision and making keynote speeches, it's about guarding the gate. You need to ask the hard questions like: "Does this person elevate what we're building, or do they just make it easier for me in the short term?"

I've seen entire departments spiral because someone made a hire to "keep the peace." I've seen A-players walk out the door because a C-player was allowed to stay, and I've felt that sting myself when I hired someone close to be my Director of Operations. If I am being honest, that was the worst hire I ever made. Not because they were a bad person or they lacked potential, but simply because lines got blurry.

This taught me a crucial lesson: Respect and relationship rarely mix in the workplace. Not when roles and results are on the line, anyway. One minute you're strategizing with someone, laying out plans, casting vision, and the next you're being told, "Bro, chill. You're doing too much."

That line right there is the crack in the dam because now, you're not leading from conviction, you're tiptoeing around connection. You're not the boss, you're the buddy who doesn't want to hurt anyone's feelings, and that's when things start slipping. You hesitate to correct, let small things slide, and before long, you're negotiating your standard in the name of keeping the relationship intact.

This is how culture doesn't just shift, it *leaks*. Not because of one big compromise, but a hundred tiny ones you never thought you'd make.

Take Shaquille O'Neal, for example. Despite his status and wealth, he's known for telling his kids, "We ain't rich. I'm rich." If you want in on anything, show me two degrees. No handouts. No inherited board seats. No "because I'm your kid" shortcuts.

That's not just parenting — that's leadership.

Leadership isn't handing out keys at family reunions; it's guarding the standard like it's sacred, and the moment proximity becomes someone's only qualification, you've already started compromising. And don't think this is just theory. Look at the trail of companies that have fallen under the weight of loyalty hires, legacy placements, and sentimental staffing. From start-ups to family businesses, empires have crumbled not from bad products, but from bad people placed in the wrong positions out of emotional obligation. Learn this: One sentimental hire can crash everything, and if that doesn't make you slow down and think about who's sitting at your table, nothing will. Now, let's look at some case studies to build up this narrative because I honestly cannot stress this point enough.

Case Study 1: WeWork – When Charisma Hires Become Culture Killers

Adam Neumann, co-founder of WeWork, was brilliant on stage—he was charismatic, visionary, and full of bold ideas. But behind the scenes, the company became a playground of unchecked behavior, ballooning egos, and zero accountability. Neumann hired friends, threw massive parties, and built a culture that prioritized hype over health. As a result, a near $47 billion valuation crumbled overnight. Billions lost, thousands laid off, and all because charisma was mistaken for capacity (Lyons, 2019). Relationship was mistaken for reliability, and when the pressure hit, the structure collapsed, because it was built more on vibes than on values.

Case Study 2: Theranos – Loyalty Over Logic

Elizabeth Holmes surrounded herself with people who believed in her dream, but few who were willing or able to challenge her. She brought in close allies, loyalists, and people who stayed silent when they should've spoken up. The company was built around protecting the illusion rather than protecting the mission. As a result, felony charges emerged, and tech unicorn turned federal disaster (Malone, 2021). All because comfort was chosen over competence.

In both of these cases, the hires weren't just bad, they were expensive. They didn't just cost money, they cost trust, credibility, and years of recovery.

Case Study 3: A Family Business Torn Apart by Nepotism

Now, a friend of mine based in South Africa told me about something similar for a company he used to work for. A regional chain of retail stores in the country was thriving under the founder's leadership until he brought his son into the COO role. The son wasn't ready, evidently lacked experience and respect for the team, but he had the name and the qualifications. Within 18 months, three top-performing executives resigned, morale tanked, and the company faced a 20% revenue drop. The founder later admitted: "I thought I was securing legacy, I didn't realize I was handing over the steering wheel to someone who hadn't earned the license."

That's what sentimental hiring does. It creates blind spots, warps judgment, and makes you ignore red flags that would've disqualified anyone else except they're "your people."

One powerful example comes from Liberty University, one of the largest Christian universities in the US. Under Jerry Falwell Jr.'s leadership, the school became entangled in a web of controversies — financial mismanagement, abuse of power, and personal scandals. But underneath the headlines was something more systemic: unchecked authority, family legacy, and loyalty hires that prioritized allegiance over accountability.

Eventually, the board had to step in. Falwell resigned, and the institution entered a long season of damage control, public scrutiny, and fractured trust — not because the mission failed, but because the leadership did.

It's a cautionary tale that transcends religion or politics. Nepotism and favoritism don't just cloud decision-making — they corrode culture. Even in value-driven organizations, when personal relationships outweigh professional standards, it's only a matter of time before everything starts to crack.

Let these stories speak louder than any leadership cliché. Leadership involves trust, so, ask yourself: Who can carry the mission without you holding their hand? Furthermore, when you're hiring, promoting, or partnering, don't just ask, "Do I like them?" Ask, "Will this person push the mission forward, even when I'm not in the room?" If the answer isn't a resounding yes, you've already made your decision because, in leadership, your silence can be the very thing that undermines your vision.

The Best Leaders Hire With Legacy in Mind

A great leader doesn't just hire for the now, they hire for what's next. They're not just building a team; they're planting seeds for succession. That's the mindset shift most people miss. You're not just recruiting for tasks, you're recruiting for torch-bearers—people who can one day carry what you started further than you ever could.

Even in ancient leadership models, the wisest leaders knew this. Moses raised up Joshua, not just as an assistant, but as a successor. And Joshua didn't just maintain the mission; he finished what Moses started. Elijah anointed Elisha, and that young prophet didn't just replicate his mentor's miracles; he doubled them. Even Jesus, arguably the most impactful leader in human history, looked His disciples in the eye and said, "You'll do greater things than I ever did." That's not just humility, that's legacy thinking.

The best leaders build with a "beyond me" mindset. They look at someone and ask, "Could this person carry the vision if I were gone tomorrow?" Would they protect the standard? Push it further? Lead with the same conviction or even more?

You see it in sports, too. Think of Phil Jackson, who didn't just coach Kobe Bryant, he mentored him to become a student of leadership. Or Bill Walsh, the legendary 49ers coach, who developed a deep bench of future head coaches by pouring into his assistants.

Business icons do this too. Steve Jobs famously mentored Tim Cook, not just as a right-hand man but as someone who could one day take the Apple vision further than he could. That's how legacy is built. Not through titles, but through transfer. Not just by keeping control but by passing the baton to someone faster, hungrier, sharper.

So, next time you're sitting across from a candidate, don't just ask, "Can they do the job?" Ask: "Do I see in them a future that's even stronger than my present?" and "Could they someday become the reason this company outlives me?" If the answer's yes, don't hesitate. That's not just a hire, that's a future anchor.

CORE VALUES:
THE FILTER YOU CAN'T AFFORD TO SKIP

If legacy is the destination, then core values are the compass. They're the silent code that governs every decision, every relationship, and every hire. And if you get them wrong, it won't matter how skilled someone is, they'll corrode your culture from the inside out.

The biggest hiring mistake is assuming you can work around misaligned values. You can't. You might try to compensate with training, coaching, or pep talks, but eventually, friction shows up, culture clashes, integrity leaks, and performance stalls because values are not "nice to have." They're nonnegotiables.

So, if you're serious about building a high-trust, high-performance team, your first filter shouldn't be the resume, it should be alignment. You should be hiring for who they are before what they do. Skills can be taught. Values? Not so much.

That's why elite leaders never settle for surface-level interviews. They don't just look for polished responses or smooth resumes. They probe. They ask questions that reach into the real story beneath the job title. This is the art of behavioral interviewing— an approach designed to reveal how a person thinks, responds, and recovers under pressure.

Instead of asking, "Can you handle pressure?", a behavioral interviewer might say, "Tell me about a moment when a tight deadline forced you to choose between delivering fast or delivering with full integrity. What did you do?" That's not just a clever question, it's a stress test. You're listening for principles, decision-making frameworks, and even emotional intelligence. You're simply trying to reveal their default wiring because that's what you're inviting into your culture.

Thankfully, technology has given us an amazing goldmine, and that is artificial intelligence. For instance, think of ChatGPT like a copilot in your hiring strategy, not replacing your judgment, but amplifying it. You can literally feed your core values into the system, whether it's accountability, creativity, ownership, or humility, and ask it to generate custom interview questions that test for those exact traits. Let's say one of your company's pillars is "taking ownership even when no one's watching." You can prompt:

"Give me five behavioral interview questions that test for personal accountability and ownership in high-stakes environments."

In seconds, you'll have questions that probe beneath the fluff, such as:

- "Describe a time when you made a mistake that wasn't immediately noticed. What did you do?"
- "Tell me about a time you took initiative to fix a problem outside your job description."
- "Have you ever had to stand up for a decision no one else agreed with? What was the outcome?"

These aren't questions you'll find in a basic HR guidebook. They're tools for cultural quality control customized to your DNA. That's the point: the deeper your questions, the clearer your hire.

You're not gambling anymore, you're qualifying and making decisions anchored in reality, not personality. Although if we're being honest, clarity alone isn't enough. This is because no amount of insight can compensate for bad timing. You can ask the right questions, run the right playbook, even use the smartest tools, but if you're asking those questions in a moment of chaos, you're already at a disadvantage.

I already said it; if you're hiring to fill a gap, you're too late. Now, here's what to do about it: Treat recruiting like prospecting. It's ongoing and intentional. Don't pick who's available now; you need someone who aligns with where the business is going. This means lunch meetings with future hires, watching for people who reflect your culture before there's even a seat at the table, LinkedIn bookmarks, DMs, soft intros, and ongoing conversations.

That's how dynasties are built—not during the off-season, but during every season. And if you don't have time to scout, build systems that do it for you. Keep a list of potential hires and create a running Google Sheet of culture-aligned prospects. Make talent review part of your quarterly rhythm because waiting until you're understaffed to start recruiting is like waiting until you're bankrupt to start budgeting.

HIRING IS LEADERSHIP, NOT HR

Ultimately, hiring isn't just a business decision, it's a leadership moment. It's not about filling seats; it's about building a legacy. Every hire is a seed you plant in the culture, the future, and the direction of your team. Get it right, and the ripple effects are generational. Get it wrong, and the costs echo far beyond payroll.

You've seen now that hiring kickass people is more than scanning resumes or asking cookie-cutter questions. It's about alignment over appearance. Hunger over hype. Integrity over smooth talk. It's knowing that assets often don't come gift-wrapped, and liabilities sometimes show up in suits.

Actually, one of the best hires I ever made almost didn't get the job. Back when I was a store manager at PetSmart, a guy named David came in to interview. To put it bluntly, it was rough. He was clearly nervous, gave short answers, and had none of the polish you'd expect from a strong candidate. If I had been hiring off the textbook, I would've easily passed, but instead of writing him off, I leaned in, changed the tempo, stopped trying to check boxes, and started trying to see the man. I asked about his life, his passions, and his story. That's when everything shifted. He lit up as he talked about hiking the entire Appalachian Trail—solo—for months. Right there, I saw it: grit, follow-through, mental toughness, and the kind of discipline that no resume can capture. I trusted my gut.

Fast forward, and he became one of the best performers I ever led. Rock solid, low ego, and high output. Years later, I wasn't the least bit surprised when he rose to store manager for another major retailer. He had it in him all along. He just needed a leader who looked deeper.

That's the game. The best leaders don't hire based on who shines under fluorescent lights, they hire based on substance. They know that diamonds are often dirty at first glance, and that brilliance isn't always loud. Sometimes the quiet ones are the ones who make the most noise once they're in the right environment.

So, as you build your team, remember that you're not just hiring workers, you're shaping the culture. You're curating the next generation and maybe even your successor.

Just like Moses raised up Joshua, Elijah poured into Elisha, and Jesus handed the mission to His disciples, great leaders look for people who can carry the baton further than they ever could. You don't just hire for function, you hire for legacy. You hire with a mindset that says, "If I disappeared tomorrow, would this person protect what we've built and push it further?" That's how dynasties are formed—not by accident, but by design.

So yes, ask sharper questions. Use tools like AI to craft brilliant filters. Hire slow and fire faster when needed, but above all, lead through your hiring. Keep your standards sky-high, your discernment sharp, and your vision long-term because at the end of the day, your company will rise or fall on the quality of the people you choose to trust with it.

With that said, we don't have time to procrastinate. Let's get to work with the Monday Morning Playbook and put all the talk into action:

MONDAY MORNING
PLAYBOOK

Your next hire will either elevate your culture or drain it.

 MINDSET SHIFT:

The worst hire is almost always the easiest one. If you're hiring out of convenience or desperation, you're building a culture of just good enough. You're not looking for warm bodies, you're building a team of assassins.

✓ DO THIS MONDAY:

1. Review Your Last Three Hires (By End of Day Today)

- **Ask yourself:** "Would I enthusiastically rehire them today?"
  - If the answer is no, write down exactly why not.
  - Identify the red flags you missed or ignored during the hiring process.
  - Look for patterns: Were you desperate? Did you rush? Did you settle?
- If you wouldn't rehire them, you've got work to do. It's either coach up or move on.

2. Audit Your Job Descriptions (By This Week)

- Pull up the last three job descriptions you posted.
  - Are they clear? Do they reflect reality, not fluff?
  - Do they scream your core values, or do they just list generic skills?
  - Ask yourself: "If a B-player reads this, will they screen themselves out?" If not, rewrite it.
- A job description should be a filter, not an invitation to mediocrity.

3. Start a Passive Talent List (This Week)

- Open a Google Sheet or Excel file. Name it "Top Talent Bench."
- List out people you'd love to work with, whether they're looking or not.
  - Past coworkers who crushed it.
  - Freelancers who showed up like killers.
  - People you met at events who had that fire.
- Great teams are built before the job is posted. Start the list today, add to it weekly.

CHAPTER 3:

STAGE ONE – ONBOARD LIKE A PRO, SET THE BAR LIKE A BOSS

"Give me six hours to chop down a tree and I will spend the first four sharpening the axe."
– Abraham Lincoln

Clarity builds confidence, systems build scale.

One of the most revealing signs of leadership failure is when a business cannot function without the constant presence of its founder. Many entrepreneurs boast about being indispensable, yet this very trait exposes a lack of systems. When a team is unable to operate confidently without daily direction, the real issue is not the people, it's the absence of clearly defined expectations and scalable processes.

Picture this: you are on a long-overdue vacation with your family, trying to unplug and recharge. However, your phone keeps buzzing. Messages flood in asking for approval, clarity, direction, or support. Some want to know how to respond to a client email, while others are still unclear on how to execute tasks you thought were already explained. You are not running a business at this point, you are babysitting one through WhatsApp.

This is not an uncommon scenario. In fact, it is a symptom of a deeper problem. When onboarding is weak and expectations are vague, the result is organizational confusion. People become unsure of what success looks like. Teams start operating based on assumptions instead of standards. Deadlines slip, morale drops, and eventually, leaders burn out trying to hold everything together.

Onboarding is not an administrative task, it is a leadership ritual. It is the moment where a company's DNA is handed over to a new team member. In the absence of structure, new hires do not step into culture, they step into chaos. Their performance becomes reactive instead of intentional. Miscommunication increases, trust breaks down, and the momentum that should be building during the first 90 days is wasted in confusion.

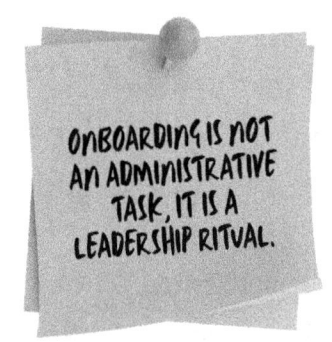

ONBOARDING IS NOT AN ADMINISTRATIVE TASK, IT IS A LEADERSHIP RITUAL.

There is a common misconception that onboarding is about filling out paperwork, getting a laptop, and sitting through a few presentations. This is an outdated view. Effective onboarding is about building alignment, clarity, and early accountability. It is about setting the tone for how people show up, what they are responsible for, and how they measure their success.

Imagine joining a sports team and being thrown into a game without knowing the playbook. You would hesitate, second-guess yourself, and likely disappoint your coach and teammates. This is exactly how new hires feel when companies fail to provide clear expectations. Even high performers underdeliver when the rules of the game are unclear. I mean, no one thrives in ambiguity after all.

The first 90 days of a new hire's journey are not just about orientation. They are about transformation. It is during this period that habits are formed, confidence is built, and early momentum is either gained or lost. When companies commit to creating systems such as 30-60-90 day onboarding plans, paired with frequent feedback and defined scorecards, something powerful happens. People begin to take ownership, they become invested, and they start thinking like leaders.

One of the most overlooked benefits of great onboarding is what it does for the founder or manager. It creates space. When your systems are clear and expectations are visible, your team does not rely on you for every small decision. You gain the ability to think strategically, rest intentionally, and lead proactively. In contrast, poor onboarding keeps leaders trapped in a cycle of re-explaining tasks, correcting mistakes, and cleaning up preventable messes.

Every business must make a choice. Either you take the time to onboard well, or you spend the time later dealing with the cost of misalignment—there is no neutral ground. Companies with high retention, strong morale, and dependable results all have one thing in common: clarity. Not just in values, but in execution.

So, in a nutshell, this chapter is designed to help you implement that clarity. You will learn how to craft onboarding plans that actually guide performance. You will discover how to use scorecards the right way without creating a culture of micromanagement. You will explore the power of early coaching, and why vague expectations are the hidden destroyer of motivation. Most importantly, you will understand why the first 90 days are the foundation of everything that follows.

If you want your business to scale beyond your presence, if you want to attract and keep top-tier talent, and if you want to lead with less stress and more strategy, then what happens in those first 90 days is not optional; it is essential.

PEOPLE SHAPE PRODUCT

When Howard Schultz returned as CEO of Starbucks in 2008, the company was losing its soul. Stores were expanding too quickly, quality had dipped, and customer loyalty was fading. However, Schultz didn't start the turnaround with a better coffee bean or a fancy ad campaign—he started with onboarding.

He shut down over 7,000 stores for a full day to retrain more than 135,000 baristas across the United States, not because they didn't know how to make a latte, but because they had forgotten why they made it the way they did. Schultz knew that if Starbucks was going to reclaim its identity, it had to start with realigning its people. He went back to the basics: how to steam milk, how to pour a perfect espresso shot, and how to deliver customer warmth with every interaction.

That decision wasn't about coffee, it was about culture. Starbucks built its empire on something far more valuable than caffeine: clarity. Every new hire is trained not just on what to do, but why it matters. Expectations are not assumed; they are embedded, reinforced, and tracked. Whether you're in Boise or

Boston, the goal is the same: create consistency in the customer experience through consistency in the employee experience. When companies get onboarding right, culture becomes scalable. When they get it wrong, even the best hires end up lost in the fog.

This brings us to one of my personal business principles that safeguard my vision: clarity is not optional; it is a kindness. Ambiguity is a leadership failure.

Remember, we already established that as a leader, if you do not define what good looks like, someone else will, and they may be dead wrong. So, you are not just hiring people; you are shaping mindsets. The first 90 days of any new hire's journey are not about watching them sink or swim. They are about giving them the map, the compass, and the support they need to swim in the right direction.

When onboarding is done right, it doesn't just train, it transforms. It's the difference between someone showing up to work versus someone showing up with purpose. That transformation doesn't happen by accident, it happens through structure one that introduces clarity, builds trust, and creates early wins.

That's where the 30-60-90 day plan steps in; not as a static checklist, but as a living blueprint. It evolves with the role, adapts to the business, and brings your expectations out of your head and into their hands. At its best, it becomes a mutual agreement—a coauthored roadmap that guides both the leader and the new hire through the messy middle of learning curves and unknowns. Think of it like scaffolding: strong enough to support real growth, flexible enough to come down when the foundation is solid.

30-60-90 DAY PLAN

One of the biggest mistakes leaders make is assuming that onboarding is just about getting someone a desk, an email login, and a warm-ish welcome on Day 1. That's not onboarding, that's orientation. Real onboarding is architectural. It's the strategic construction of a launchpad. The 30-60-90 framework didn't appear out of thin air, it's been a staple in leadership development for decades, championed by performance experts, corporate consultants, and even military officers who understand that progress follows structure. It gained major traction in business literature thanks to Michael Watkins, who popularized it in his book, *The First 90 Days*. His research showed that leaders who had a clear roadmap for their first three months were significantly more likely to succeed in their roles and avoid early burnout or political landmines.

What started as a tool for executives quickly became a gold standard for any role, in any industry. From start-up environments to enterprise giants like Amazon and GE, this framework has become a proven way to accelerate ramp-up time, set clear expectations, and create accountability from day one.

A 30-60-90 plan brings three things every new hire desperately needs but rarely asks for:

- Clarity – What exactly am I here to do?
- Direction – How do I prioritize my time?
- Feedback Loops – Am I on the right track?

When people don't get those answers early, they fill the void with anxiety, assumptions, or apathy. The plan eliminates that drift and provides structure without smothering autonomy. It builds confidence without inflating egos and, best of all, it creates alignment between employee and leader before confusion creeps in.

The Anatomy of 30-60-90

Each phase of the plan has its own rhythm and objective:

Days 1–30: Learn & Absorb

This is the onboarding immersion phase. The focus here is on understanding the business, the team culture, the tools, and the systems. You don't just teach people what to do, you teach them how the organization thinks.

Key goals:

- Learn company values, product offerings, and customer pain points.
- Sit in on meetings, shadow team members, and ask a lot of questions.
- Get access to systems, tools, dashboards, and everything they'll use daily.
- Build relationships. Culture is contagious, but only if you breathe it in.

Days 31–60: Contribute & Test

By now, the hire should be moving from observation to contribution. This phase is about applying what they've learned, taking on small projects, and getting some wins under their belt.

Key goals:

- Execute tasks with guidance. No more hand-holding, but still some coaching.

- Get feedback on quality, speed, and communication.
- Begin developing routines and systems for efficiency.
- Start owning parts of meetings, reporting, or decisions.

Days 61–90: Own & Elevate

The final phase is about ownership. This is where leaders should be able to say, "They've got it." At this point, expectations should be clear, and performance should be measurable.

Key goals:

- Own projects or outcomes independently.
- Bring ideas to the table. Challenge processes with insight, not ignorance.
- Demonstrate consistency, reliability, and alignment with company values.
- Start mentoring others who are newer or struggling—the culture now flows through them.

Small Biz? No Problem. Big Enterprise? Even Better.

Whether you're running a lean five-person content studio, a midsized law firm, or a multinational logistics operation with hundreds of employees across time zones, the 30-60-90 plan scales. That's the beauty of its plug-and-play system—it adapts to your business stage and budget, while still delivering structure and alignment.

If you're a start-up or small business, you might not have a dedicated HR department—or even an HR person—but that's not a barrier. Tools like Basecamp, Notion, or Google Docs make building and tracking a 30-60-90 plan incredibly easy and cost-effective. They require no fancy software, no lengthy onboarding of their own, and they integrate with tools you're probably already using. You can literally drag-and-drop action items, tag teammates, add due dates, embed training videos, and create progress boards all in one place. These tools are especially powerful for small teams because they allow everyone to stay aligned without needing formal systems. Furthermore, since early-stage companies evolve quickly, your onboarding needs to flex. Roles expand, job descriptions shift, and workflows change on the fly, and that's okay. Let your plan breathe, evolve, and get sharper with each hire. The structure is the skeleton, but the muscle grows through iteration.

Now, for midsize to enterprise-level companies, this needs to be more formal. It's not just about clarity anymore—it's about consistency at scale. That's where real onboarding systems come into play. Think SAP SuccessFactors, Workday, BambooHR, or Greenhouse—all designed to manage onboarding workflows, track performance, and automate follow-ups across departments and even continents. These tools help HR teams assign tasks, schedule check-ins, collect feedback, and integrate KPIs straight into the onboarding lifecycle. A well-configured HR system ensures that everyone gets the same quality of onboarding experience, whether they're in New York, Nairobi, or New Delhi. It also makes performance measurable from Day 1, linking your 30-60-90 plan to probation reviews, role competencies, and long-term growth conversations.

The Evidence Is Loud and Clear

If you're still unsure whether onboarding deserves this level of attention, the numbers are hard to ignore. A Gallup report showed that only 12% of employees strongly agree that their organization does a great job of onboarding new hires. That's shockingly low and costly. Poor onboarding is a leading cause of early turnover, disengagement, and lost productivity.

On the flip side, organizations that implement structured onboarding processes see 82% higher retention rates and over 70% increases in productivity. Not theory, data. Companies that take onboarding seriously don't just keep people longer, they unlock their potential faster.

A great 30-60-90 plan doesn't feel like a to-do list handed down from the mountain. It's not just about assigning tasks, it involves setting direction, clarifying purpose, and creating space for the new hire to co-own the journey. As the plan progresses, it should become increasingly two-way. The hire reflects on what's working, what's unclear, and where they feel confident or stuck. They begin suggesting improvements, noticing process gaps, and asking sharper questions. That's how you know it's working—it's no longer a checklist, it's a conversation. A real one about growth, trust, and excellence.

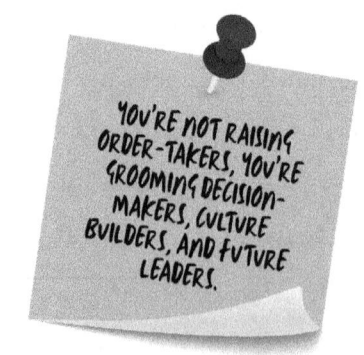

The ultimate goal isn't compliance, it's ownership. You're not raising order-takers, you're grooming decision-makers, culture builders, and future leaders. Now that's what a 30-60-90 day plan done right really is.

Now that you understand the strategy behind 30-60-90 onboarding, here's a sample layout to help you get started. Think of this as a foundation you can adapt for any role, whether you're hiring a junior designer, a sales closer, or a logistics coordinator. The key is to customize it based on the role, your culture, and your current business needs.

Start here, tweak as needed, and make it your own.

30-60-90 Template Example

Let's assume the role is: Customer Success Representative (clean, relatable, and covers multiple skills like communication, systems, and processes).

First 30 Days: Orientation & Learning

Goal: Understand the business, the tools, the customers, and the culture.

Focus Area	Actions	Metrics / Milestones
Company & Product	Complete product training. Attend team meetings. Shadow top reps.	Finish onboarding modules. Pass the product quiz.
Tools & Systems	Learn to use CRM (e.g., HubSpot), support tools, and ticketing systems.	Set up profile, test workflows.
Culture & People	Meet key team members. Join 1:1s with the team lead and peers.	Attend five intro meetings. Join Slack channels.

Reflection Questions:

- What are our customers' biggest pain points?
- What part of the system feels unclear or intimidating?

Days 31–60: Execution & Engagement

Goal: Begin handling tasks with light supervision. Focus on learning by doing.

Focus Area	Actions	Metrics / Milestones
Customer Interaction	Respond to tickets, emails, and customer inquiries.	Resolve 10–15 tickets/day with a 90% rating.
Internal Process	Log calls, tag issues, and escalate appropriately.	Complete 100% of follow-up tasks.
Feedback Loop	Join biweekly feedback sessions with a mentor or manager.	Receive two documented coaching sessions.

Reflection Questions:

- ☐ Where do I feel confident now?
- ☐ What systems/processes still feel unclear?

Days 61–90: Ownership & Optimization

Goal: Operate independently. Identify areas for improvement.

Focus Area	Actions	Metrics / Milestones
Autonomy	Handle full ticket load. Suggest process improvements.	95% SLA hit. One improvement idea shared.
Reporting	Track own KPIs and identify trends in customer issues.	Submit one mini-report to the team.
Team Collaboration	Participate in team training or lead a micro-workshop.	Host an internal session or write a help article.

Reflection Questions:

- Where can I go above and beyond in this role?
- How can I support newer team members?

Ultimately, a solid 30-60-90 plan is like GPS for a new hire—it doesn't just say "go," it shows how to win at their role, week by week. Furthermore, when people know what the destination looks like, they stop asking for directions and start taking the wheel.

So, now that we've mapped the road, let's talk about the rules of the road—setting clear expectations and defining nonnegotiables.

We've already discussed what excellence looks like, but now it's time to anchor that excellence in writing because great teams don't just vibe—they align.

Setting Clear Expectations & Defining Nonnegotiables

A 30-60-90 day plan is only as strong as the expectations behind it. You can have the most beautifully designed onboarding blueprint in the world, but if the expectations are unclear or they keep shifting, you're setting your team up for confusion, frustration, and missed targets. Clarity, at this stage, isn't a luxury; it's leadership.

Great teams don't succeed by accident, they operate with clear playbooks, shared definitions of success, and unshakable standards. Likewise, new hires don't come into your company with a mind-reading superpower. It is your job to define what good looks like. And once that's done, your job is to protect that definition with discipline. Nothing erodes a new team member's confidence faster than hitting a target only to find out later it was the wrong one.

This is where nonnegotiables come in. These are the cultural guardrails that define your operational DNA. They're the standards that hold weight even when things get busy, even when performance is high. Whether it's punctuality, responsiveness, quality of communication, or how customers are treated, your nonnegotiables are the backbone of your company's rhythm. Let's break this down clearly:

Category	Clear Expectation	Nonnegotiable Standard
Communication	All internal emails are responded to within 24 hours	No ghosting. No passive-aggressive silence.
Meetings	Weekly team sync every Monday at 10 a.m., no exceptions	Show up on time. Come prepared.
Customer Interaction	Weekly team sync every Monday at 10 a.m., no exceptions	No customer is ever left wondering what's next.
Quality Control	Every deliverable goes through peer review before delivery	Sloppy work is never "good enough."
Ownership	If it's your task, it's your responsibility	No blame-shifting. No excuses.

These aren't suggestions, they are standards. Once you define them, you must defend them because once the goalposts move, trust breaks and when it does, performance drops also. Remember how we discussed that when expectations are unclear, people don't feel empowered—they feel anxious then they begin to hesitate, second-guess, and check in too often. That's how you end up micromanaging, not leading.

Most leaders don't set clear expectations because they think it's too "rigid" when in actual fact, clarity doesn't stifle creativity, it unleashes it. When people know exactly what's expected, they stop wasting mental energy trying to decode the unspoken rules. Instead, they focus on execution. They take initiative and they innovate inside the lines.

Think of it like a jazz band. Every player has room for expression, but they're still playing in the same key, on the same rhythm, moving in the same direction. That's what clear expectations create: a shared tempo.

Finally, let's address the worst thing a leader can do during onboarding, which is to change the rules mid-game. You can't say one thing during the interview, train them on something slightly different, and then six weeks in, demand something completely different. That is a fast track to disengagement. It's like being told to run a marathon, training for it, and then halfway through being handed a swimming cap.

So instead, define the game from the beginning, set the rules, set the tone, set the nonnegotiables, then stick to them. After all, high-performing cultures are not built on vibes; they're built on standards, and standards only work when they're clearly set, clearly communicated, and consistently enforced.

One final example, when you walk into a Ritz-Carlton, you're not just paying for a bed and a breakfast, you're paying for an experience; a predictable one. That predictability isn't accidental, it's engineered into every layer of the business through what they call "The Gold Standards."

One of those standards is that every employee, regardless of rank, is empowered to spend up to $2,000 to solve a guest's problem without needing approval (Toporek, 2022). That's not just a perk, that's trust, with structure, because behind that freedom is a set of meticulously trained expectations that every employee knows by heart. From bellhop to general manager, the staff are onboarded into a shared understanding of excellence: how to greet a guest, how to solve issues, how to think proactively rather than reactively.

New hires aren't left to "figure it out," they're immersed. They don't just learn what to do, they learn why it matters, how it fits into the larger vision, and how it reflects the brand's DNA.

Furthermore, the results speak for themselves. The Ritz-Carlton has become a gold standard in hospitality not just because of its buildings, but because of its people that are shaped by a system that defined expectations from day one (*CX Recovery Tactics: Ritz-Carlton's $2K Empowerment Rule and Its Impact O,* 2025).

That's what you want to build: a culture where excellence isn't improvised, it's repeatable. Where your team doesn't need micromanaging, because the standards have already been hardwired into the system. You don't need marble floors and $2,000 gestures, you just need clear expectations, consistent onboarding, and the discipline to reinforce your nonnegotiables.

You've set the stage. The role is clear. The expectations are defined. Nonnegotiables are on the table. Now comes the part most leaders hesitate with—but the great ones embrace: accountability.

Accountability involves creating clarity, consistency, and care. When done right, accountability becomes the *culture*. It's the quiet current that powers great teams, not the electric fence that shocks them into compliance.

Think about it: What's the point of onboarding someone with vision and values, only to let those values fade in the day-to-day grind? Accountability is how you keep the standard alive *after* the welcome emails stop. It's what separates teams that plateau from those that rise.

Great leaders don't just set the bar, they *keep* the bar. You made a promise to your team when you hired them that this would be a place of excellence. Following through on that promise means having the courage to call out drift and the care to call people back into alignment.

Let's break down how to build a system where accountability feels empowering, not punishing.

Accountability

Accountability is not micromanagement...

Let's kill a myth right now: Holding your team accountable is not the same as hovering over them like a paranoid boss with trust issues.

Micromanagement is checking in every five minutes, questioning every move, making people feel like they're toddlers with sharp objects. That's control or even insecurity and honestly, it's a recipe for burnout for you and them. Accountability, however, is something else entirely. That's adulthood at work. That's saying: "Here's what we agreed on, here's the deadline, I expect it done. If it's not, we're talking."

That's it. No drama, no spying, just straight expectations. The best teams don't need babysitters, they need clarity. And when you give people clarity, and they still drop the ball, guess what?

You're not wrong for calling them out, you're actually wrong if you don't.

If you're not holding your people accountable, you're not leading, you're either babysitting, or worse, hiding.

Accountability is not a "nice-to-have." It's your damn job. It's part of the deal you signed up for when you said, "I'll lead" because what you tolerate, you endorse, and what you ignore, you empower. Every missed deadline you let slide, every excuse you nod at every underperformer you "give another chance" without consequence, you're telling the rest of the team: "This is okay here."

Here's what typically goes wrong:

- Lack of clarity: You can't hold someone accountable for what was never clearly communicated.
- Inconsistency: One team member gets away with murder, the other gets a performance review for showing up five minutes late.
- Fear culture: If feedback always feels like punishment, people will hide their failures, not fix them.
- No follow-through: Expectations are set during onboarding and then forgotten by month two.

It's like buying a new iPhone and never updating the software. Everything slows down, glitches, and crashes. Accountability is the system update your team needs.

Also, accountability shouldn't be event-based. If your only moment of accountability is during the annual performance review, you're doing it wrong. That's like checking your parachute after you've jumped out of the plane. Instead, create accountability rhythms, predictable check-ins, scorecard reviews, one-on-ones, and project debriefs. These are your alignment meetings.

This is structured time that makes your team feel seen, supported, and responsible. Rest assured, people crave this, high performers want feedback. They want to know where they stand. The only people afraid of accountability are those coasting under the radar.

Build the Machine - When Accountability Becomes Culture

This brings us to a deeper point about how accountability is communicated. It's not just about what's said, but how it's said. One of the most powerful approaches comes from Kim Scott's framework called "Radical Candor." The premise is simple but profound: Care personally, challenge directly. That means as a leader, you don't sugarcoat hard truths, but you don't weaponize them either. When a team member drops the ball, the conversation isn't, "You're not good enough." It becomes, "Here's the impact of what happened. I know you're capable of more, and I want to help you get there." That's accountability laced with dignity. It builds people rather than breaking them.

One founder I deeply admire has a rule etched into his company culture: "If you see it, you own it. If you own it, you fix it." There's no buck-passing, no hiding behind titles or hierarchy. In his organization, accountability is everyone's job because the mission is everyone's responsibility, and when everyone takes ownership, momentum becomes unstoppable.

Now, the most beautiful evolution of accountability is when it no longer relies on the leader. That's when it becomes embedded in the culture. Great teams eventually start policing themselves, not out of fear, but out of pride. They care too much about the mission to let mediocrity slide. They notice when standards slip, and they call each other out, not to shame, but to sharpen.

You'll hear it in passing:

"Hey, you missed that deadline. Is everything okay?"

"That's not how we show up; let's clean that up."

"This isn't our standard, let's do better."

That's when you know you've built something special. The culture starts enforcing itself, and that's when your leadership stops being about control and starts being about influence.

Think of Navy SEAL units or elite firefighting crews. They don't wait for the commander to correct sloppy execution, they step in mid-mission because they understand the cost of poor performance. They're driven by something deeper than compliance, they're driven by commitment. That same energy can be built into your business if the vision is clear, the standards are high, and the team feels deeply invested in both.

Of course, even in the healthiest cultures, mistakes happen. People mess up, and that's just a normal part of being human. What separates mature leadership from reactive management is how we respond to those missteps. Correction must be swift, but not harsh. The goal is never to humiliate but to realign. Start early, before dysfunction calcifies. Speak to behavior, not identity— "You missed the mark" is different from "You're not reliable." Create space for dialogue. Ask, "What's getting in the way?" and then listen. End every hard conversation with a clear, practical next step. That's how you turn a stumble into a stepping stone.

Also, don't forget to model the same thing yourself. Every once in a while, let the team hear you say, "That one's on me. Here's how I'll fix it," because nothing teaches accountability more than a leader who lives it.

One of the greatest business examples of trust-driven accountability comes from Toyota. In their legendary production system, they introduced the Andon Cord—a literal cord that any worker, at any time, could pull to stop the entire assembly line if they noticed a defect (Geraghty, 2022). Now think about that: A junior employee, on the spot, can halt a billion-dollar operation because quality matters more than speed. That's not just a system—that's a culture that says, "We trust you. You are responsible, and your standards shape the final product."

Most companies would never dream of empowering their people to that degree. Maybe that's why most companies will never reach Toyota's level. Accountability doesn't kill speed; it builds trust, and when it is scaled, becomes your ultimate competitive advantage.

Which brings us to the next layer of culture-building: how you give and receive feedback.

Feedback

The first few weeks of someone's journey in your team are where your culture is most fragile and most moldable. If you get lazy here, you don't just miss a teaching moment—you miss the moment where expectations crystallize. This is the reason why, if you aspire to become a great leader, you should be prepared to coach proactively, not reactively. For instance, great musicians don't wait for the concert to tune their instruments; they check their pitch constantly. Same goes for high-performing teams, so as a leader, your job is to tune the culture, and feedback is the key.

Early on, this can look like short daily check-ins with new hires:

- What are you working on today?
- What got finished and what's outstanding?
- Any questions or challenges?

No need for long meetings, just quick morning or evening briefings are enough for you to guide, support, and reinforce expectations before bad habits start forming. This also normalizes feedback as part of the rhythm, not just a spotlight during failure.

No one hits a target they can't see. So, your feedback should consistently point to a clear standard of excellence. It's not enough to say, "Do better." Show them what better looks like. For example, let's say a new designer submits a campaign that feels a little off-brand. You don't just say, "This doesn't work." You say: "We're aiming for clean and bold. Think more Apple, less cluttered. Let's lean into whitespace and storytelling. You're close—just polish the edges." That kind of feedback sharpens, not shames. It tells them you're paying attention, you care, and you believe in their ability to rise.

Also, feedback should flow both ways. One-sided feedback cultures don't last. If your team is only ever receiving and never giving, you've got a communication gap, not a culture. The strongest teams have leaders who regularly ask:

- "What's getting in your way?"
- "Where am I dropping the ball as your leader?"
- "What can we improve in how we work?"

That posture models humility, builds trust, and creates a safe environment where feedback becomes mutual; not just managerial so when your team starts giving you feedback, don't flinch, welcome and acknowledge it as well. That's when you know your culture's alive.

Now, the most elite feedback cultures don't rely on quarterly reviews to fix everything; they have rituals, small, consistent structures that ensure nothing drifts too far from the center. Here's one example that's simple but powerful:

Weekly 1-on-1s (30 Minutes Max)

- 10 min – "What are you proud of this week?"
- 10 min – "Do you need anything from management?"
- 10 min – "What support do you need from me?"

This rhythm makes feedback predictable, safe, and normalized. No surprises, just two intellects getting aligned and sharpening each other week in, week out. Once you learn this approach, you start to realize that feedback isn't an attack, it's an investment.

Feedback on Repeat – Make It the Air Your Team Breathes

Let me get personal for a moment. One of the most effective tools I've ever implemented in building strong teams wasn't some fancy AI system or overpriced leadership course. It was this simple principle: give feedback early, give it often, and make it normal.

It might sound extreme to some, but I believe in catching the moment while "it's still fresh." I've even taken a page (or two) from how Ray Dalio built Bridgewater Associates. Now, I'm not saying we record every meeting or rate each other live with a "dot collector" like they do, but I've adopted the spirit behind it: radical clarity.

I make it a norm to call things out in real-time with love, but with precision. If something's off, we don't let it slide. If something's great, we spotlight it and dissect why it worked. As a result, people adjust quicker, there's less drama, less second-guessing, and more momentum. Once this rhythm becomes part of the culture, people stop fearing feedback and start craving it because they know it's not personal, it's directional. We aren't chasing perfection, it's all about progression.

That's why I coach hard in the early stages. I push for clarity in the moment, not six weeks later in some performance review no one remembers. I treat feedback like a muscle—not a weapon. You don't have to run a hedge fund to install this mindset, but if you want a team that runs without chaos and confusion, start there: Make feedback normal and make clarity sacred. When you do, performance becomes predictable, and that's where scorecards come in.

Using Clear Metrics to Guide Early Wins

I don't create scorecards because it's "good HR." I do it because I hate wasting time, money, and energy on the wrong expectations.

A scorecard is the contract of clarity that says: "Here's what winning looks like in this role. Not vibes or effort but outcomes." When done right, it becomes the north star of early performance. Forget the long onboarding plans with dozens of checkboxes. I just want to know:

1. What must this person crush in their first 30-60-90 days?

2. What behaviors are nonnegotiable?

3. How will we both know if they're actually killing it?

If we don't agree on that, we're playing a dangerous game of guess and hope. For instance, let's say I'm hiring a Marketing Lead. Their scorecard might include:

- Launch 2 campaigns in 60 days with X% engagement target

- Own weekly content cadence without hand-holding

- Create a reporting system that leadership trusts by Day 45

Now, imagine I sit down with them in Week 2 and ask: Which one of these feels most clear and which one's fuzzy?"

Now we're actually coaching, not micromanaging.

Furthermore, a static scorecard is a waste. What makes it powerful is how often it's revisited. I recommend three core touchpoints:

1. Day 1 – Scorecard Walkthrough: "This is the game. Let's win it together."

2. Weekly – Tactical 1:1s: "Where are we tracking green? What's yellow or red?"

3. Day 45 – Mid-Onboarding Gut Check: "Are you feeling momentum? Do you know where you stand?"

When those convos are normal, you never need to guess whether someone's performing, and they never have to guess either. Scorecards don't just help top performers fly—they help you spot misalignment early. I've had hires where, by Day 30, we're already seeing the gap. They're trying, but not delivering. In the past, I might have kept hoping. Now, I pull out the scorecard and say: "You're putting in effort, but here's what we agreed matters. Let's talk about what's working and what's not." Sometimes, that convo saves the hire, and other times, it shows you both that it's not the right fit. Either way, you lead with clarity, not chaos. So, let the scorecard build the culture, not just the role. That's when you get a performance-driven, trust-filled team. That, my friend, is the foundation of your greatness.

Key Performance Indicators

Once expectations are clear and your scorecards are built, there's still one essential question left: How do we actually measure progress? This is where KPIs come in as the sharp tools that keep your team accountable and your business on course.

In simple terms, KPIs *(key performance indicators)* are measurable values that tell you if the work being done is moving the company toward its goals. They originated from the battlefield of scale. As companies grew, founders couldn't keep track of every detail. So they focused on the signals—those numbers that would either whisper early warnings or shout success. Every great company has them, and every great operator respects them.

However, KPIs involve more than just gathering data, they enhance alignment. They turn scorecards into dashboards. They give your team feedback loops they can see and respond to in real time. When done right, KPIs eliminate guesswork and fuel performance.

Without KPIs, your leadership turns into a guessing game. You start relying on feelings instead of facts. One day, it feels like the marketing team is crushing it until you realize leads are down 40% this quarter. Or someone seems "busy" every day, but when you zoom out, the actual output is flatlining.

KPIs anchor your observations in data. For instance, they help you with the following:

- Spotting trends before they become problems
- Coaching people with clarity, not emotion
- Keeping conversations grounded in outcomes, not effort
- Separating movement from progress

However, not all metrics are created equal. Some just make you feel good, and in all honesty, these are vanity metrics. They look impressive on a slide deck, but they don't drive meaningful results. For example:

- Website traffic isn't the same as qualified leads.
- Task completion isn't the same as value delivered.
- Social media likes don't equal customer acquisition.

Then vital metrics, on the other hand, tie directly to results. They answer the real questions:

- Are we growing?
- Are we efficient?
- Are we serving our customers well?
- Are we improving over time?

If a KPI doesn't tie back to a core objective on your scorecard, it's just noise. Let's say your scorecard for a Customer Success Manager includes a goal like: "Increase customer retention rate to 90%."

A KPI that supports that goal might be:

- Net Promoter Score (NPS)
- Number of customer check-ins per month
- Churn rate over time
- Time-to-resolution on customer issues

These KPIs help you and your team members measure whether their daily work is actually moving the needle toward that retention goal. They make the invisible visible. That's the beauty of KPIs: they pull the curtain back and let you *see* what's working and what's not, early enough to act.

A few rules to keep your KPIs tight and useful include:

- Focus on 3–5 key KPIs per role or per objective.
- Choose KPIs that can be measured consistently (weekly or monthly).
- Use them in your rhythms—weekly meetings, monthly reviews, 1-on-1s.
- Make sure your team understands them, owns them, and knows how to improve them.

Also, teach your team how to read their own numbers. Don't let KPIs become tools *you* use to evaluate them. Let KPIs become tools *they* use to evaluate themselves. That's when the magic happens.

Let's bring this home with a practical breakdown. Below is a simplified example of a scorecard with its connected KPIs for a Sales Representative:

Scorecard Objective	Key KPIs	Measurement Frequency
Close $100,000 in new business per quarter	Total Closed Revenue	Weekly / Monthly
	Average Deal Size	Monthly
	Win Rate (% of proposals closed)	Monthly
	Pipeline Coverage Ratio (3x Target)	Weekly

	Outbound Calls/ Emails per Week	Weekly
	Demos or Sales Meetings Booked	Weekly

This table provides clarity. Your rep knows exactly what winning looks like—and you know how to coach them when they're off-track. Instead of vague conversations about "working harder," you now have specific metrics tied to specific outcomes. So, in short, great leaders don't just set expectations; they create feedback loops. KPIs are the radar, the mirror, and the fuel. They make performance visible, measurable, and manageable. They help you steer the ship before it crashes into the rocks. Don't get lost in the data; KPIs should serve your mission, not become the mission. Keep them lean, keep them relevant, and always tie them back to the outcomes that matter. You can't control what you don't track, and you can't grow what you don't measure.

Operating Rhythms

Throughout this journey, we've established that performance is influenced by more than giving orders or quarterly strategy docs; it's the daily, weekly, and monthly rhythms. The drumbeat, the cadence, the rituals that quietly set the pace and expectations for your entire organization. Operating rhythms ensure alignment, drive accountability, and create a natural feedback loop without needing micromanagement. These are intentional systems that answer questions such as: "How often do we check in on what matters most?" Perhaps we should look at examples of how great leaders build operating rhythms that actually work.

Daily: Tight Loops for Clarity & Momentum
- Morning Huddles (10-15 minutes briefings)
- End-of-Day Wraps (Optional, 5 minutes)
- Leadership Pulse Check: Even just a quick Slack check-in or tap on the shoulder lets people know you're present.

These daily loops keep people focused, remove ambiguity, and build momentum.

Weekly: Scorecard Reviews, Wins & Wobbles
This is where the metrics meet the mission. Each week, teams should review their scorecards/KPIs to track:
- What's on track?
- What's off track?
- What's stuck?

These are mainly for decision-making moments, and they're powerful when led right. Use them to:
- Celebrate wins
- Triage issues early
- Realign priorities

When you do this consistently, people start to correct themselves before things spiral, and that's cultural maturity.

Monthly: Strategy, Reflection & Reset
Monthly rhythms zoom out a bit:
- Revisit strategic goals
- Celebrate milestones
- Analyze trends from the KPIs

- Tackle larger cross-functional problems
- Gather feedback and listen

This is your recalibration window. Like taking your car in for servicing. You don't do it because it's broken, but because you want it running at its best.

Ultimately, every step you take is healthy and positive enough to keep your rhythm strong, which in turn ensures priorities stay clear, accountability becomes expected, communication flows both ways, and morale stays high because people feel seen, heard, and aligned. Most importantly, problems never get to fester. Issues are surfaced and solved while they're still small, which becomes a game changer.

Most of the time, I've learned what great leadership looks like by experiencing the opposite. Years ago, I joined a small catering and vending company as a General Manager. It was a huge pivot leaving big-box retail (Target, Dick's Sporting Goods, PetSmart) for the world of small business. I wanted more control over my time and a path beyond retail.

But I wasn't ready for how broken the basics were.

First day; no welcome, no plan, just a laptop with no login info. When I asked for help, I got an irritated sigh and a scribbled Post-it note. That was it. That HR director never even coached or followed up or showed any sense of care whatsoever. It became clear that if I was going to make it, I was on my own. That experience taught me everything not to do.

Today, onboarding is sacred. I build detailed 30-60-90 day plans. I show up on day one with intention and clarity. I coach and check in daily that first week. Not just because it's good practice but because I remember what it feels like when no one does. You only get one shot at a first impression, so make it count.

So, forget the jargon—it's time to lock these principles into your core. Let them guide you until they become second nature. Obey them religiously, because trust me, they'll save you a hell of a lot of pain down the road.

First off, clarity without action is just noise, and now that you've got the blueprint for setting standards and calling things out in real-time, it's time to make it muscle memory. That's exactly what this week's Monday Morning Playbook is designed to do: turn accountability into instinct and feedback into fuel. Let's get to work.

MONDAY MORNING
PLAYBOOK

Again, you only get one shot at a first impression. Great onboarding builds trust, clarity, and momentum from Day One. Confusion won't be on them, that's on you.

🧠 MINDSET SHIFT:

Ambiguity kills culture, whereas clarity builds confidence. Your new hire shouldn't have to guess. Your job is to set the goalposts and keep them there.

✓ DO THIS MONDAY:

1. Pick One Role on Your Team and Review Their Onboarding (Today)

- Choose one role, preferably one where you've seen inconsistency.
- **Ask yourself:**
  - Does the onboarding include a 30-60-90 plan?
  - Are expectations clearly defined and written down?
  - Is there a feedback loop baked in from Week One?
- If any of these are missing, you've left them to guess. Rewrite it, clarify it, execute it.

2. Ask Your Newest Team Member These Three Questions (Today)

- Find the newest hire on your team and ask them directly:
  - "What's unclear about your role right now?"
  - "What do you think 'great' looks like here?"
  - "What would make your onboarding feel more helpful?"
- Shut up and listen. If they hesitate, push them: "No, I want the real answer."
- Write down their feedback. If there's confusion, it's on you.

3. Create or Refresh One Scorecard (This Week)

- Pick one role and build a scorecard with 5–7 KPIs that are simple, trackable, and tied to results.
  - This is not busywork, it's the blueprint.
  - Review it weekly. If they're missing targets, it's visible. If they're crushing it, it's known.
  - Make it a tool for coaching, not punishment. Clarity drives confidence.

CHAPTER 4:

CRACK THE CULTURE CODE – BUILD A PLACE PEOPLE NEVER WANT TO LEAVE

"The strength of the pack is the wolf, and the strength of the wolf is the pack."

– Rudyard Kipling

There's this guy I used to know, let's call him TK.

He was one of those entrepreneurs who made noise early. Visionary, charismatic, and had that whole move fast and break things energy that made people want to follow him. However, somewhere along the way, the "vision" got so loud, he stopped listening. The company grew, the team expanded, but he never really adjusted. He thought that because he said something once, everyone got it. He assumed his energy would somehow leak into the culture without him needing to define it.

Then his Head of Sales started bending the truth to close deals. Just slightly. A little overpromise here, a little delay in delivery there. TK heard about it and shrugged. "As long as we're hitting numbers."

A month later, customer complaints started trickling in. A few key employees left. Then more. Internal trust started quietly dissolving, one unresolved tension at a time. But hey—revenue still looked decent on the outside.

By the time TK realized the cost, it wasn't just about bad apples; it was about a garden that hadn't been tended. No roots, no rituals, no real standards—just vibes. He learned it the hard way that vibes don't scale; that's the trap. Culture doesn't collapse overnight. It erodes slowly, in the tiny decisions leaders dismiss.

Culture isn't what you claim. It's what you tolerate. It's what spreads behind your back, and if you're not intentional about building it, chances are very high you won't like the result. You can serve a cheeseburger at home, and you can walk into

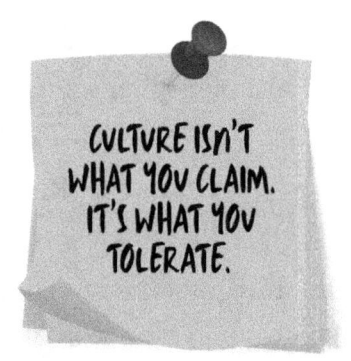

CULTURE ISN'T WHAT YOU CLAIM. IT'S WHAT YOU TOLERATE.

McDonald's and get one too. Same ingredients, yet totally different experience. Why? Systems, rituals, expectations—unspoken cues that shape behavior without needing to micromanage it. That's the power of culture. It takes something ordinary and turns it into something repeatable, scalable, and predictable. Trust me, in business, predictability is gold.

A good culture creates clarity, loyalty, and momentum. It's the difference between a team that performs because they have to, and one that performs because they want to. Unfortunately, most leaders spend weeks crafting strategy decks and barely an hour thinking about culture. They chase metrics but ignore moods. They architect visions but let culture "just happen," and when it's left to chance, strategy eventually breaks, talent leaves, and vision cracks under pressure.

You can't fix culture when it's already broken; you build it before it's tested, and if you've been in the game long enough, you know that it definitely will be tested. So, we've been throwing around this word culture like it's universally understood, but what are we actually talking about?

We say sports culture, start-up culture, pop culture, then we talk about "company culture" like it's this mysterious force, yet most people couldn't define it if their paycheck depended on it, and ironically, it kind of does.

In simpler terms, culture is just the spoken or unspoken collective agreement about what's normal, what's rewarded, and what's off limits. It's how people behave when no one's watching. It's what gets laughed at, what gets praised, what gets ignored. It's the emotional climate, the invisible algorithm running in the background (Valenzuela, 2023).

You don't need posters on the wall to have a culture, you already have one. The only question is—did you design it, or did it design itself?

So, this time around, we need to make sure you're not leaving that answer to chance. Let's break down what a culture code actually looks like without the unnecessary slogans; just honest, usable frameworks that shape your team at a cellular level. If you can get this part right, the rest becomes so much easier.

CULTURE

You walk into a church for the first time. Nobody knows you. You're not wearing a suit. You sit in the back, quietly. The sermon hasn't even started yet, but in less than 10 minutes, you already feel what kind of church this is.

A stranger shakes your hand with real warmth. Someone else slides over to make room for you. There's laughter during announcements. Not performative, not polished—just... sincere. You hear someone pray out loud in the row behind you, not because it's on the program, but because it felt right. Nobody's forcing anything. Nobody's faking anything. Now pause, did anyone give you a brochure explaining the church's "culture"? Did you sit through a PowerPoint presentation before service? Nope, but what you felt—that's culture. Culture doesn't need to *announce* itself. It *reveals* itself.

The same thing happens in offices, restaurants, start-ups, and even families. You walk in, and within minutes or sometimes seconds, you know whether this is a place of pressure or peace. Control or trust, chaos or rhythm, whether people are surviving or thriving, because culture is what happens when no one's performing. When the script runs out and people act on instinct. That instinct is what your culture has trained, intentionally or accidentally. So, you don't build culture by writing about it. You build it by living it, enforcing it, and sometimes, by firing the people who violate it.

Furthermore, culture is shaped by the things we celebrate, the behaviors we repeat, and the lines we draw when no one else is watching. It's formed in the tension between what we say we value and what we actually allow. The danger is; culture doesn't form at once, it drifts. Slowly, quietly, one compromise, one exception, and one ignored red flag at a time.

It's not always dramatic either. Sometimes, it's subtle—a new hire who's great at the job but sucks the energy out of the room. Or a manager who keeps winning clients but burns through team morale like jet fuel. If you're not careful, these moments harden into muscle memory, and once a culture adapts around dysfunction, it gets harder to reverse. That's why so many organizations only realize the culture was broken when it's already too late. Let's look at how this plays out in the real world—in boardrooms, in break rooms, and in billion-dollar companies that figured out what many leaders ignore, which is: *Culture doesn't cost you, lack of it does.*

Take SAS Institute, a quiet giant in the analytics space. While most companies scramble to offer trendy perks to boost retention, SAS built something deeper and far more enduring: a true culture of care. They didn't just add benefits as an afterthought; they baked humanity into the operating system of the company itself. At SAS, support is proactive, not reactive. On-site childcare, comprehensive healthcare, wellness programs, flexible work hours—these aren't "perks" dangled like bait, they are expressions of a core belief that employees are whole people, not just units of productivity. Leadership doesn't just tolerate work-life balance; they champion it. Managers are trained to care about the personal well-being of their teams. Facilities are designed to reduce stress, from green spaces to fitness centers. Communication is open and accessible, promoting trust rather than fear. The cultural message is clear: "You matter here, your family matters, your health matters, and your peace matters." This kind of environment creates more than loyalty—it breeds emotional ownership. People don't clock in and out just for a paycheck; they invest their energy because they know they are invested in it. They feel safe enough to take creative risks. They feel supported enough to weather challenges. They feel trusted enough to lead from wherever they are.

The result is industry-low turnover, high engagement, and quiet, consistent innovation. SAS isn't known for flashy marketing campaigns or loud headlines, but it has built a place where talent doesn't just stay, it flourishes. In a world obsessed with chasing talent, SAS quietly proves that the real key is keeping it, by creating a workplace where people want to build their lives, not just their careers.

Culture like that can't be manufactured quickly; it can't be copied by offering a few bonuses or launching a wellness initiative. It's the byproduct of years of intentional leadership, grounded in the simple but radical idea that if you put people first, performance will follow.

Now consider W. L. Gore & Associates, the innovative minds behind GORE-TEX. Instead of traditional titles and rigid hierarchies, they built something far more powerful: a "lattice" structure where leadership isn't assigned, it's earned. You're a leader at Gore if people choose to follow you, not because a title demands it, but because your actions inspire trust and confidence.

Influence is organic, rising naturally from credibility, collaboration, and contribution (Amazing Workplaces, 2023).

This approach isn't loose or chaotic, it's trust turned into structure. By removing unnecessary layers of authority, Gore frees people up to own their work fully. Accountability becomes personal, not just positional. Initiative is encouraged, not micromanaged. As a result, employees are taught through experience, not just slogans, to act like owners. And ownership always outperforms compliance, because people protect, nurture, and elevate what they feel truly belongs to them.

At Gore, culture isn't a set of rules etched on a plaque; it's a living system that rewards initiative, builds mutual trust, and unlocks potential in ways rigid systems rarely can. It's a reminder that when you trust people with freedom, they often reward you with greatness.

Or take Zappos—a company so obsessed with culture that they would actually pay you to quit if you didn't fit in. Seriously. After onboarding, new hires are offered cash to walk away. Because culture isn't just shaped by who joins; it's defined by who stays. At Zappos, employees were given freedom, fun, and above all, a deep sense of purpose. The result was fanatical customer service, a raving customer base, and a business model that didn't just succeed, it became a legend (Benton, 2022).

Then there's Nvidia, a tech powerhouse with a culture that would make some leaders sweat. High-performance, high-accountability. CEO Jensen Huang reportedly still has hundreds of people reporting directly to him, a staggering number by traditional standards (Tenney, 2022). It's intense, but it's not toxic. The reason behind this is that their culture is mission-first and ego-last. At Nvidia, never mind who gets the credit; it's about advancing the mission. People push hard because the mission pulls harder. There's no need for artificial motivation when the purpose itself is that compelling. That clarity of purpose acts like a magnet, drawing in top talent and aligning their energy toward shared goals. In a place like this, the bar is high, but the reward is the deep satisfaction of building something truly world-changing together.

Such a culture is felt, tangible, and measurable. When it's strong, people don't just know what to do, they want to do it. That kind of internal alignment can't be bought, it must be built. You can copy systems and even clone strategy, but culture; that's the force you can't fake.

Now, to build culture, you need a system, a playbook that makes your values actionable, visible, and unmissable, and that's where culture frameworks come in. These are intentional systems that turn beliefs into behaviors. They shape how people treat each other, how decisions are made, and how problems get solved, even when leadership isn't in the room.

Frameworks for Building a Living, Breathing Culture

Whether you are leading a company, a church, a school, or even just a small team, the principles stay the same: Culture lives or dies by what you deliberately build into the system.

So, let's look into some of the strongest, most practical frameworks you can use to build a culture that is not only inspiring but also functional and lasting. These are proven patterns that organizations across industries have used to create environments where people thrive, loyalty compounds, and excellence becomes the standard.

CODE OF CONDUCT

Every thriving culture has unwritten rules that shape behavior long before official policies ever get mentioned. Great organizations, great teams, even great families, eventually realize that to protect their identity, they have to go further. They codify their expectations in simple, living documents that feel more like promises than laws.

Without that clarity, confusion creeps in, standards blur, and energy leaks. The right people start feeling uncomfortable, and the wrong people start feeling empowered. Remember, culture doesn't collapse overnight, it erodes in slow, invisible ways.

Look at the U.S. Military. Before any soldier touches the battlefield, they are trained, retrained, and immersed in a Code of Conduct that shapes instinct. Loyalty, integrity, honor, and accountability—these values are the invisible armor that protects the mission when pressure hits.

Even schools naturally build Codes of Conduct. Churches build them. Start-ups, even before their first round of funding, begin to shape themselves, whether they realize it or not. If you don't intentionally create a Code of Conduct, you accidentally create one through what you tolerate and excuse. Either way, a "culture document" is being written every day by your actions.

A strong Code of Conduct doesn't exist to control people; it exists to protect the atmosphere where the right people can thrive. It sets clear, proud expectations from the start, leaving no room for confusion when standards are later upheld. By drawing a firm line early, it prevents drift, preserves momentum, and attracts those who are serious about excellence.

Practical: Building a Living Code of Conduct

- **Start Simple.** Write a one-page document describing "How We Act When No One Is Watching." Focus on behaviors, not just beliefs.
- **Tie Actions to Outcomes.** Instead of vague statements like "Be respectful," show what respect looks like in real life (e.g., "We respond to messages within 24 hours" or "We confront issues face-to-face, not over gossip").
- **Teach It, Don't Just Post It.** Review your code quarterly with your team—not to criticize people, but to recalibrate together. Let it be a living conversation, not a stale plaque on a wall.
- **Live It Loudly.** Praise public examples of people living the code, not just quoting it. Turn "culture wins" into everyday storytelling moments.
- **Update It as You Grow.** As your team evolves, your Code should evolve too. Keep it true, keep it fresh, and stay ruthless about protecting its spirit.

In the end, your Code of Conduct isn't just a list of rules. It's a lighthouse. When the storms of busyness, stress, and rapid growth hit—and they will—the Code is what keeps your culture off the rocks. It reminds everyone who they are, what they stand for, and what "winning" looks like around here, even when the pressure is high.

Build it early, guard it fiercely, and let it become the silent coach that keeps your culture sharp when no one's looking.

RITUALS

Culture without rhythm fades. Rituals are the steady pulse that keeps it alive. They take the values you believe in and weave them into the daily fabric of how your people think, move, and interact.

Powerful cultures aren't built on random sparks of energy. They're forged in consistent, meaningful actions, small moments that, over time, shape identity more than any memo or mission statement ever could.

Think of the difference between a spark and a campfire. A spark flares once and vanishes. A campfire stays alive because someone keeps feeding it, tending it, and protecting it. Rituals are how you feed the fire of your culture every day.

Take IDEO, the legendary design and innovation firm. Creativity isn't just encouraged at IDEO—it's protected by daily rituals. For instance, at certain offices, employees set aside sacred times called "design critiques," where teams gather to give each other honest, constructive feedback on works-in-progress. It's not a side note it's built into the workday.

No "boss says so." No HR reminders. It's a living, breathing part of the culture because IDEO knows that without rhythm, even the best values wither into slogans.

Same thing happens in great churches: weekly prayer meetings aren't just events, they become anchor points that renew identity. Same thing in great companies: daily huddles, quarterly off-sites, Friday shoutouts, anniversary awards. The point isn't the event itself. The point is to reinforce who we are, how we move, and what matters here. When you get rituals right, they don't feel forced, they feel familiar, comforting, and empowering. They carry your culture when words fail.

Practicals: Building Rituals That Matter

- **Identify Key Values First.** Rituals must serve a value, not just fill a calendar. For instance, if "radical candor" is a value, create a monthly "truth-telling" session where feedback is celebrated.
- **Make Them Visible, Not Optional.** Rituals must be public enough that everyone sees and feels them, not hidden in back rooms or buried in admin calendars.
- **Keep Rituals Alive, Not Robotic.** Evolve rituals over time. If something becomes stale, update the format but keep the spirit alive.
- **Celebrate Micro-Wins.** Rituals aren't just for big moments; celebrating small behaviors that reflect the culture keeps momentum alive day by day.
- **Rituals Are Greater Than Rules.** A rule might correct behavior once, but a ritual rewires it permanently. True culture change isn't achieved by controlling isolated moments; it's built by creating lasting momentum.

Every great band has a drummer. Not because drums steal the spotlight, but because they set the beat everyone else can follow. Without that steady rhythm, even the best musicians start to sound like noise. Culture works the same way. Rituals set the beat. They turn your team's energy into something powerful, aligned, and unforgettable. Furthermore, they don't just maintain culture; they multiply it. They take the invisible values on your wall and carve them into the muscle memory of your people. Still on carving things deep... let's talk about *symbols*—how the smallest things (a desk, a badge, a T-shirt) can scream your culture louder than a thousand meetings.

SYMBOLS

You can tell a lot about a team without hearing a single word. Sometimes it's in the way desks are arranged, sometimes it's the way someone wears a branded hoodie like it's a badge of honor. Other times, it's in the parking lot where the founder still parks out back, even when there's a reserved spot by the door.

That's the quiet power of symbols. Culture isn't always spoken, it's signaled, and symbols are those quiet, consistent signals that speak louder than speeches ever could. They're physical, visible reminders of what matters, what gets honored, what gets remembered, and what gets repeated.

Walk into Apple's headquarters and everything, from the minimalist design to the obsessively clean glass panels, tells you something about how seriously they take simplicity and excellence. That's not an accident, that's culture, reinforced visually.

Or think of Patagonia. The recycled materials in their lobby, the activist posters on the walls, the bike racks everywhere, they're not decorations, but they're declarations.

These small things preach louder than handbooks. They shape behavior without saying a word. Symbols can be physical objects, repeated phrases, or signature moves. Maybe it's a gong you hit when you land a big deal. Maybe it's a handwritten note from the CEO on your work anniversary. Maybe it's how the top leaders always take the last seat at the table, not the first. These actions may not require formal policies, but they shape the atmosphere.

So, if symbols carry that much cultural weight, don't leave them to chance. Here are a few simple ways to start using them intentionally:

- Audit your space: What does your office, Zoom background, or Slack channel *say* without words?
- Create visible artifacts of wins: A "Wall of Firsts," a digital bell, a public shout-out system.
- Eliminate symbols that contradict your values: Fancy perks with no purpose, VIP treatment that undercuts humility, etc.
- Introduce new ones with meaning: Design team jackets, a team mantra wall, or a ritual object passed down during onboarding.

Symbols shape the environment, but it's the invisible atmosphere that shapes behavior. You can decorate your office with values, but if people don't feel safe to speak up or challenge ideas, your culture is just surface-level branding. Let's talk about the foundation that makes innovation, trust, and real teamwork possible—psychological safety.

Psychological Safety – The Culture of Courage
The greatest threat to any culture isn't laziness. It's fear.

Fear of speaking up.

Fear of being wrong.

Fear of being the first to go against the grain.

You'll never build a culture of innovation if your people are scared to raise their hands. Think about Peter in the Bible—yeah, the same guy who stepped out of the boat in a storm. Say what you want about him sinking, but at least he got out of the boat. That's psychological safety. Jesus didn't shame him for sinking. He reached down and pulled him back up. That's leadership. That's how people learn to take bold steps, not by being punished when they fail, but by being covered when they try.

Now, bring that into the workplace. Imagine a junior team member has a wild idea during a strategy meeting. It's rough around the edges, not fully thought through but it's bold, it's fresh. What happens next determines your culture. If the leader says, "That's not how we do things," or even gives that subtle eye roll? Game over.

But if the leader leans in and says, "Walk me through that… let's unpack it," now you've just greenlit innovation. Not just for that employee, but for everyone watching.

Take note, however, that psychological safety doesn't mean people get to slack off or say whatever they want without consequences; it means people know they won't be embarrassed, blamed, or shut down for bringing ideas, asking questions, or calling out problems. It's safety, not softness.

When Satya Nadella took over Microsoft, the company was siloed, political, and dominated by internal turf wars. People kept their heads down. Failure meant humiliation, but Nadella flipped the script. He introduced a growth mindset culture, he didn't reward people for always being right, he rewarded learning, risk-taking, and cross-collaboration. Microsoft went from stagnant to one of the most valuable companies in the world, not because of a new strategy, but because they had smart people for years. He changed the emotional climate.

This proves that people don't shut down because they lack intelligence, they shut down because the room feels dangerous to their ego, their future, and to their dignity.

In psychologically unsafe cultures, people become professional pretenders. They agree too quickly, nod too often, and leave their best ideas at home. What's worse is that they watch others fall and keep quiet, because the environment rewards silence over truth.

That's why the smartest leaders don't just run meetings, they orchestrate emotional safety. The best ones speak last. They ask questions like, "What's your view on this?" and then go silent. Not fake-silent, but real-silent, long enough for the quieter voices to surface. It's not a technique, it's a discipline.

In one team I coached, a manager began every weekly sync with this phrase: "Whose perspective might I be missing?" You'd be shocked at how fast that changed the air in the room. Suddenly, interns spoke up, engineers suggested product tweaks, and essentially, people just leaned in so easily.

So, it's the invisible rituals that speak the loudest. Public celebration of courage—not just performance—is another one. A bold idea that fails still gets airtime. A mistake owned in public becomes a learning badge, not a black mark. When someone admits, "I got that wrong," the room doesn't tense up; it breathes out. That's a sign you're building something rare.

You want to go further? Install a simple language that people can use to flag disagreement safely. A designer I worked with once introduced the phrase, "Can I lovingly challenge that?" into her team culture. It caught on. Disagreement didn't feel like war, but it felt like collaboration. And when failure shows up—because it will—what you say first matters. If the first question after a mistake is "Who dropped the ball?" you've already shrunk the room, whereas if it's "What can we learn here?" you've just created space for growth. The best leaders don't waste failures, they repurpose them.

The final move then becomes to model it. Model the hell out of it. You want your team to be real? Start by being real first. I've watched entire teams open up after their leader said three words most execs choke on: *"I don't know."*

COMMUNICATION CADENCE

Every strong company has a rhythm—not just a mission, but a heartbeat. That rhythm comes from how consistently your team communicates, aligns, and connects. This is what we call communication cadence—the recurring, predictable beats that shape how information flows, how trust builds, and how priorities stay clear even in chaos.

Think about any high-performing group: a band, a Formula 1 pit crew, even a military unit. They don't wing it every day, they operate on rhythm, sync, and patterns. It's not robotic—it's intentional. When cadence is off, confusion enters. When it's tight, there's flow.

In business, communication cadence isn't about how often you talk, it's about how intentionally you create space for connection. It's the tempo of your trust, and just like music, the wrong tempo can kill the vibe. Too fast and your team feels overwhelmed. Too slow and they drift into disengagement. However, hit the right beat and you create momentum, accountability, and culture that feels alive.

This isn't theory, cadence shows up in the real world in how the best teams never miss a beat. Consider NASA's launch teams, before every mission, they run simulations with set communication protocols. Each person knows when they're supposed to speak, what data to give, and how decisions flow. Ambiguity kills rockets, whereas clarity launches them. The same is true in your company. Chaos doesn't come from lack of ambition, it comes from lack of rhythm. A team that doesn't communicate well becomes a band playing different songs at the same time. Loud? Yes. Productive? Not at all.

So, what are the drumbeats you need to set?

The Weekly 1-on-1: Sacred Space

Too many leaders treat 1-on-1s like optional check-ins—a box to tick. However, in healthy, high-performing cultures, this meeting becomes sacred and not only because of what's on the agenda, but because of the intent behind it.

A top founder I once advised used to open every 1-on-1 with just one question: "Is there anything on your mind that you haven't said out loud yet?"

That single line unlocked breakthroughs, emotional honesty, and retention. People didn't leave that company because they felt heard, and being heard beats being paid more somewhere else.

It doesn't require a fancy framework, but it does require discipline. A consistent rhythm—same time, every week, without cancellations unless it's critical. Over time, these meetings become mirrors. A place for pulse checks, coaching, accountability, and personal growth.

Here's a simple 1-on-1 flow that scales with any leader:

- Check-in: How are you doing, really?
- Feedback loop: What's working? What's not?
- Growth pulse: What's one thing you're learning?
- Alignment: Are we still rowing in the same direction?

Do that 50 times a year and you'll outperform leaders who throw money at engagement surveys while remaining emotionally unavailable.

All-Hands: Not a Presentation—a Cultural Reset

If 1-on-1s build intimacy, all-hands meetings build energy and alignment. They are your cultural amplifier not only because you present performance charts, but because you remind people why it matters. If done well, they become the monthly heartbeat of the company. Unfortunately, many founders use them as a broadcast only. "Here's what we did, here's what's next." Snooze. The best ones turn them into bonfires, a moment of shared story, a spotlight on effort, and a reflection on the journey—not just the numbers.

Take Duolingo. Their CEO, Luis von Ahn, once opened an all-hands by sharing a funny customer review and how it sparked a whole product revamp. It wasn't scripted, it was real. Indeed, it was real to the point that it created a culture of listening, iteration, and humility.

Your team doesn't want a slideshow. They want a signal: "Are we still in this together?" They want to see your eyes, hear your tone, and feel that you care.

Just one tip that's worked wonders for me: end every all-hands with 10 minutes of "wins from the field." Let different teams share small victories as this creates a rhythm of shared success and reinforces the idea that no win is too small to celebrate.

The Rhythm Is the Culture

These rituals—1-on-1s, all-hands, and yes, even leadership team meetings (which we've discussed earlier)—are the scaffolding of culture. They don't feel flashy or exciting on a whiteboard but they shape your team's heartbeat.

Let me give you a different kind of case study I came across about the world-famous Manchester United. In the early 2000s, when Sir Alex Ferguson rebuilt Manchester United's dynasty, he didn't just focus on strategy or talent. He focused on rhythm. Every Friday, he'd walk into the locker room and ask his players about their families. He wasn't focused on performance or results but on personal stuff, and every Monday, he'd do a 15-minute "reset talk" that had nothing to do with tactics and everything to do with mindset. That rhythm built trust, trust built belief, and ultimately, belief built dominance.

The same principle holds true in business. Your rhythm teaches your team:

- How often we talk.
- How honest we are.
- How feedback flows.

- How recognition happens.
- How we show up when things get hard.

Rhythm becomes the culture, and when your rhythm is off, so is your culture. Here's the twist though: the best rhythms don't feel like cultural activities, they feel just natural, invisible, and embedded. It can manifest in very simple ways, such as:

- A CEO sends a 90-second Friday recap video filmed from their phone to share lessons from the week.
- A team starts every stand-up with a question: "What's one win outside of work?"
- A department head sets a rhythm of "last-10% honesty" where people are encouraged to say what they're afraid to.
- A manager rotates meeting facilitation, so everyone gets practice leading the room.
- A sales team does 5-minute "Story Fridays," where one rep shares the story behind their toughest win.

These are intentional moments repeated often enough that they become who you are.

CULTURE-AMPLIFYING TOOLS

Every app you adopt, every system you normalize, every habit you reward—they either become an echo of your values or a quiet betrayal of them. And the real kicker? Most leaders don't even realize this is happening until it's too late. Culture shows up in tone, timing, attention, and yes, in the tools we use to scale communication, recognition, feedback, and clarity. So, we're not talking about "Which project management app is hottest this year?" We're digging into something deeper: How do we deliberately choose tools that turn invisible values into audible rhythms?

When your company's heartbeat isn't felt, people drift. When your leadership voice becomes mechanical, people stop listening. So, the tools you use either amplify your intention or muffle it.

Picture this: you start a team huddle every Monday. It's just 10 minutes on Zoom. No big slides, just real talk. You open with, "Here's what's in my heart this week," or "Here's where we're winning," or sometimes, "Here's where I blew it." That's not just a meeting, that's a tool. It's shaping how people see feedback: vulnerability, alignment, and momentum. If you ever stop showing up for it, the void will speak louder than any tool you ever implemented.

See, culture isn't just written on the wall, it's typed in Slack, spoken in voice notes, and implied in what goes unanswered. It's revealed in the breadcrumbs of how you build.

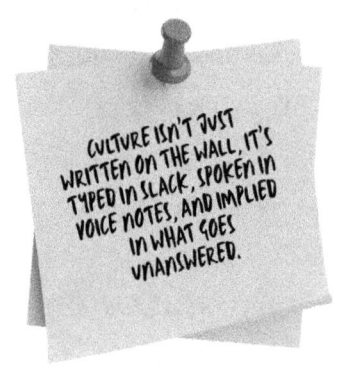

Now, let's talk about intelligent amplification. As your team grows, you can't be in every room. You can't coach every moment live. That's where tools *can* become powerful partners—if you're intentional.

When used right, they don't just scale your operations. They scale your empathy.

- You want more reflection? Build in weekly prompts on a rhythm tool like 15Five, but don't automate your response. Let people feel *heard*.

- You want to normalize recognition? Don't create a "shout-out" channel just for decoration. Use it, show up, and be the loudest celebrator.

- You want to decentralize clarity? Then make the knowledge base sacred but never silent. Review it, update it, and treat it like a living trust.

A well-used Loom can carry your conviction across time zones, and a Slack thread can set culture just as much as a town hall. A Google Doc with values documented and challenged can preserve identity long after you're in the room. However, none of these tools work on their own; they reflect you. That's the raw truth. Tools are not shortcuts; they're mirrors and whatever they reflect, people believe.

I want to give you a cheat sheet that doesn't just name the tools, but matches them to values. Not to copy, but to inspire.

Cultural Value	Reinforcing Tool	Why It Works
Radical Transparency	Loom, Notion, Public Threads	Turns updates into narratives, knowledge into trust.
Rapid Feedback Loops	Slack Threads, 15Five	Surfaces friction before it festers, normalizes micro-adjustments.
Recognition & Energy	Bonusly, Shoutout Channels	Makes praise visible, emotional, and contagious.

Psychological Safety	Weekly Retro Prompts, Google Forms	Gives space to speak the truth without fear.
Growth & Development	Lattice, Custom Career Map	Connects ambition to reality, coaching to metrics.
Speed with Sanity	Asana, ClickUp, Slack Emojis	Keeps priorities visual without obsessing over process.
Thoughtfulness	Voice Notes, Memos, Docs	Prioritizes context and tone over rushed replies.

Pick 2–3 tools that match your real values, not your competitors', then build habits around them. Remember, don't expect tools to create culture; expect them to reinforce it.

That said, even the best tools only go so far. Systems can set expectations, and symbols can whisper values, but sustaining culture—truly sustaining it—requires more than mechanics. It requires leaders who can read the room without a script. Leaders who know when to challenge, when to pull back, and when to push forward, not based on a manual, but on the individual in front of them. That's where leadership moves from being operational to becoming personal. Let's explore what it means to lead with precision, not just policy.

INDIVIDUALIZED LEADERSHIP: THE ART OF SEEING PEOPLE

You don't lead a team, you lead individuals.

Each person you manage is a unique equation: background, talent, triggers, insecurities, aspirations, and learning style. When leaders ignore that, what you get is one-size-fits-all leadership:

shallow, clunky, and ineffective. What you want instead is bespoke leadership—the kind that adjusts not by lowering standards, but by shifting the lens.

Think of Phil Jackson, the legendary coach of the Chicago Bulls. He didn't coach Dennis Rodman the same way he coached Michael Jordan. Rodman was unpredictable, wild, intense; he needed space to be himself and still feel protected by the system. Jordan, on the other hand, thrived under pressure and wanted to be challenged, sharpened, and called higher. Jackson didn't apply "fairness" by treating them the same. He practiced equity by giving each what they needed to bring out their best.

That's individualized leadership. It means you study your team, not to control them, but to serve them.

This doesn't mean babying people or becoming their therapist, it means asking sharper questions, such as:

- What fuels this person's motivation?
- How do they receive feedback: blunt, detailed, gentle, or visual?
- Are they drained by public attention or energized by it?
- Are they ambitious and under-challenged, or overwhelmed and hiding?

One of the biggest mistakes leaders make is rewarding everyone the same way. For one person, a cash bonus feels like love. For another, a shout-out in front of the team triggers anxiety. For someone else, time off is the best reward you could ever give them. If you don't know that, if you don't ask, you'll keep offering steak to a vegetarian.

So, I've come to understand that leadership maturity is realizing your team's diversity is not a problem to manage, but a palette to paint with. Take time to notice patterns. Who responds well to tight deadlines? Who freezes under pressure but soars with autonomy? Who thrives with collaboration versus solo work? Who's secretly bored and too polite to say it? You'll be shocked how much opens up when your team realizes you actually see them. That they're not just part of a unit, they're known, understood, and led accordingly.

Take time to *notice* patterns. Who responds well to tight deadlines? Who freezes under pressure but soars with autonomy? Who thrives with collaboration versus solo work? Who's secretly bored and too polite to say it?

You'll be shocked how much opens up when your team realizes you *actually see them*. That they're not just "part of a unit"—they're known, understood, and led accordingly.

That leads us into some real-world, practical coaching:

Tailoring Your Leadership

SITUATION	BAD LEADERSHIP	INDIVIDUALIZED APPROACH
A team member is underperforming	Scold publicly or micromanage	Ask: Is it a capability issue or a clarity issue? Adjust coaching accordingly.
You need to give feedback	Same tone, same style for everyone	Learn how each person best receives correction, and adapt delivery.

Celebrating wins	Monthly shout-outs in a team email	Customize rewards: lunch with the CEO, extra PTO, public praise, or a handwritten note.
Onboarding a new hire	Generic checklist, same buddy system	Pair them with someone who shares their working style or background—create cultural safety fast.
Motivating during tough seasons	Push harder with generic pep talks	Reflect on individual motivators: some need clarity, some need vision, and some just need rest.

You're not expected to be a personality expert or motivational guru. However, you are expected to care.

To slow down enough to notice.

To ask enough to understand.

To lead well enough that people grow because of you, not around you.

Furthermore, there's another dynamic that accelerates this kind of culture: the ability to inject lightness and joy into the daily grind without losing focus or edge.

The Power of Play: Gamification

Work doesn't have to feel like a grind to be serious. In fact, the best teams often find ways to make progress feel like play. Not childish games, but smart systems that tap into what drives people: challenge, feedback, reward, and progress.

When used right, gamification doesn't water down performance. It unlocks it. Think about how we respond to games in our everyday lives. Fitness trackers reward consistency with streaks, language apps show your progress in levels, and credit cards offer tiered perks. These systems all tap into the same core wiring, which we're motivated by visible progress and small wins, especially when they connect to a meaningful goal (The Investopedia Team, 2021).

Business works the same way, and if you want your culture to thrive, you've got to inject elements of play that make excellence feel exciting, not exhausting.

Let's break that down with some clear applications:

- Create shared goals that rally the team, not pit them against each other. This isn't about "who sells the most" but "how much can we grow together?" For example, if your whole team hits a certain monthly KPI, they unlock a shared reward—a special off-site day, a team dinner, or even just a fun Zoom happy hour with a twist.

- Build in progress mechanics. Think punch cards, digital leaderboards, or monthly scorecards where people can track wins. Make the metrics visible and easy to understand. The objective isn't to embarrass low performers but to help everyone see where they stand and where they can grow.

- Inject surprises and creativity. One company built a BINGO board for internal development activities—attend a workshop, give feedback, mentor a peer, close a deal. Each row cleared unlocks a mini reward. Another leader randomly drops a mystery gift every Friday to someone who embodies the company values that week. It keeps things fresh and values-focused.

- Let the team shape the game. If your people help design the challenge, they'll buy into it far more deeply. Ask them: What would be a fun way to recognize growth? What kind of prizes would actually matter? You'll be surprised how often the prize isn't the reward itself, it's the sense of progress and recognition.

Gamification, when rooted in your actual culture and not gimmicks, reinforces everything you're trying to build: ownership, clarity, motivation, and shared energy.

To help you craft your own systems, here's a snapshot to reference:

Gamification Tactic	What It Does	Why It Works
Shared Team Challenges	Builds cohesion over competition	People root for each other instead of racing against one another
Scorecards & Visual Tracking	Makes progress and gaps visible	Feedback loops are faster, clearer, and more empowering
Surprise Recognition or Rewards	Keeps morale fresh, fun, and values-aligned	People love being noticed, especially when they least expect it
Development BINGO or Task Games	Encourages well-rounded growth and initiative	Turns soft skills into something concrete and actionable
Team-Driven Design of Challenges	Increases ownership and creativity	When people help build it, they believe in it more deeply

Smart leaders know that work and joy don't have to compete. When you design a culture that takes excellence seriously and brings fun into the equation, your people stop clocking in—they start buying in. And this beats compliance every time.

Recognition That Resonates

We've touched on recognition a lot not as a gimmick, but as a thread that runs through onboarding, rhythms, feedback, and leadership itself. That said, before we conclude this discussion, it's worth pausing because when you see someone—*really see them*—and you name the values they've embodied, you reinforce the culture you're trying to build. You remind people not just what they do, but who they're becoming and why it matters. Sometimes the smallest moments are the most lasting ones, such as a note, a nod, a timely word that says: *I noticed*. That's how you build cultures that remember their people—and people who'll never forget their culture.

CULTURE IS A LIVING CODE

In a nutshell, culture isn't a mural on the wall, and it's not the team lunch or the mission statement laminated in the breakroom. What is it, then? It's the unspoken language of your workplace that is written by your behavior as the leader. You can build culture with precision, care, and consistency. You can install feedback loops, run brilliant onboarding, create killer scorecards, and celebrate wins. Unfortunately, though, all of that can be unraveled in a moment if the leader isn't willing to embody the very thing they preach. I learned that the hard way.

During my time as COO of a prominent engineering firm, my role extended far beyond operations. I was, in many ways, the emotional buffer for a CEO who struggled deeply with empathy and emotional control. He saw collaboration as weakness, questions as disrespect, and team input as threats. When I arrived, the culture was hemorrhaging. Employee NPS scores were abysmal. Trust was nonexistent, and you could feel the fear in every meeting.

So, we went to work, rolled out EOS, clarified roles, introduced rhythms, and gave people a voice. And slowly, the fog began to lift: laughter returned to meetings and departments found pride again. This signaled that culture was healing.

Then it happened.

On a routine leadership call, our Director of Engineering offered a thoughtful (and reasonable) idea, but the CEO didn't like it. With zero warning, he snapped:

"Shut the fuck up and stay in your lane."

The call went dead silent. By morning, she had resigned and honestly, I didn't try to stop her. Now, what came next was worse: the CEO didn't apologize. He doubled down and said she was out of line and it was deserved. In that moment, a year's worth of trust vanished.

Directors went quiet, Slack channels slowed down, and ownership disappeared. The message was clear: *No system can protect you from a culture that's ruled by fear.* I stayed a little longer than I should have, but eventually, I left with a scar that became a philosophy: Culture is built on trust. And trust can be broken in a sentence.

So, always remember this:

All the playbooks, structures, and processes in the world mean nothing if the leader can't lead with character. If people can't feel safe, they won't grow. If they can't be heard, they'll stop speaking, and if they don't trust you, they'll never give you their best. Culture is not a fixed asset, it is living, breathing, and fragile. Treat it like the sacred ecosystem it is, and it will reward you beyond measure.

So, now you've got the tools and you've got the frameworks. Now, it's time to turn insight into action. Let's break down exactly how to implement what you've just learned with actionable, Monday-ready steps that help you transform culture from theory into reality.

MONDAY MORNING
PLAYBOOK

Culture isn't your logo, your mission statement, or your ping-pong table. It's how people feel working with you. It's how they act when they're not being watched and what they expect from each other when they are. If you're not owning it, you're letting it own you.

🧠 MINDSET SHIFT:

Your culture already exists. The question is: Are you owning it or avoiding it? You don't get to opt out. Whether you're intentional or not, you're building culture every single day.

✓ DO THIS MONDAY:

1. Book a One-on-One with Your Most Honest Team Member (Today)

- You know who it is, the one who's not afraid to call it like they see it.
- Ask them: "If you were me for a week, what's the first thing you'd change about our culture?"
- Then shut up and listen. Don't justify, don't push back, just absorb.
- Write down what they say. If it stings, that's a good sign, it means you're getting the truth.

2. Audit Your Communication Cadence (This Week)

- Pull up your calendar. Look at your 1-on-1s and leadership meetings.
  - Are your 1-on-1s happening every week without fail?
  - Are your leadership meetings actually solving problems or just recapping the obvious?
  - Are your updates clear, consistent, and transparent?
- If the answer is no to any of these, fix it now. You can't build a strong culture on shaky communication.

3. Post One Core Value Publicly This Week, Then Live It

- Choose the most relevant core value and put it up where everyone can see it.
  - Slack, Whiteboard, email—whatever your main communication channel is.
- Call it out when someone embodies it, and celebrate it publicly.
- If your values aren't visible and actionable, they're just words. Make them real.

CHAPTER 5:

COACHING & GROWTH – HOW TO DEVELOP A HIGH-PERFORMING TEAM

"You don't inspire your teammates by showing them how amazing you are. You inspire them by showing them how amazing they are."
– Robyn Benincasa

There comes a point in every leader's journey where the numbers stop being the biggest problem. It's no longer about driving more revenue, launching a new feature, or acquiring the next client. Instead, the real bottleneck becomes the people, or more accurately, their growth. You begin to realize that the true difference between an average team and a high-performing one is not how well they follow orders, but how well they develop. This shift in mindset is what separates managers from leaders. Remember, earlier we agreed that managers keep systems running, whereas leaders build people. In all honesty, if you're not developing your team intentionally, you're slowly draining the potential out of your organization.

Many leaders make the mistake of thinking that growth will happen naturally if they just hire the right people. They assume talent alone is enough, while potential without development is like raw ore that never gets refined; it looks promising from a distance, but is useless under pressure. Growth doesn't happen on autopilot, it must be engineered, nurtured, and reinforced. It's not a bonus you offer your team when things are going well; it is the very responsibility of leadership itself. Your role isn't simply to maintain performance, then—it's to unlock the next version of each person under your care.

This requires more than performance reviews or occasional pats on the back. It demands consistent coaching, tailored feedback, and an ongoing commitment to helping people stretch beyond their comfort zones. Leadership that avoids this work may produce short-term results, but it will always plateau. People will either stagnate or leave, and when they do, they take untapped potential with them, the kind of potential that could have been transformed into leadership, innovation, and long-term momentum had someone just taken the time to develop it.

To illustrate this, imagine a blacksmith in ancient times: he doesn't simply hand out swords to his warriors. He builds them. He heats the raw metal, hammers it into shape, tempers it, and then sharpens it, stroke by stroke. Each blade must be forged with care, pressure, and purpose. Once it's complete, it's not just stronger, it's prepared. A raw chunk of iron may look solid, but it won't survive a battle. The warrior's edge depends on the blacksmith's fire.

That's what real leadership looks like. You're not here to hand out tools and hope your team wins the fight, you're here to forge them. To take what's raw and promising and transform it into something resilient and refined. This is how good teams become great, and how great ones stay sharp enough to lead the way.

COACHING IS THE NEW LEADING

Most managers are trained to chase performance. They measure output, monitor deadlines, and react when results slip. And in fairness, performance matters. But if that's all you ever measure, you end up managing for maintenance, not growth. You keep the lights on, but you never build something brighter.

Leadership, real leadership, isn't just about execution; it's about elevation. It's about seeing potential in people before they see it in themselves, and choosing to invest in that potential over and over again. That's what coaching is: it's the difference between having a workforce and building a force. You can have a team that hits their KPIs or a team that outgrows them. One version is transactional, whereas the other is transformational. And that transformation doesn't come from a quarterly meeting or a motivational talk but from consistent, intentional coaching-week after week, one conversation at a time.

Great leaders don't just push for output, they pull out potential. That's why the real shift isn't from manager to leader anymore, it's from leader to coach. In the past, we applauded the transition from being a boss to becoming a leader, and rightfully so. That evolution mattered.

Quick recap: We've gone over how a boss gives orders, but a leader provides direction. A boss uses authority; a leader builds influence. That step forward changed workplace culture in meaningful ways, but today, it's no longer the final frontier of leadership; it's just the entry point. Nowadays, your people don't just want clarity or inspiration, they want development. They don't want to simply be managed better, they want to be invested in. They want growth, feedback, stretch assignments, real-time support, and a future that feels attainable. Leadership that motivates but never mentors isn't enough. If your leadership style doesn't produce transformation, then it's falling short. This is where coaching becomes essential.

Leadership sets direction, coaching builds capacity.

Leadership casts vision, coaching creates pathways.

Leadership says, "Let's go," coaching says, "Here's how we grow."

The best leaders today act like world-class coaches. They don't need to dominate the field, but their fingerprints are on every play. They study behavior, recognize blind spots, provide constant adjustments, and tailor their feedback to the individual. They don't just celebrate results, they cultivate potential. Where others see raw talent, coaches see responsibility to refine it. Coaching is not about having all the answers, it's about asking the right questions, creating the right structure, and giving your people the support, challenge, and belief they need to evolve. A true coach doesn't settle for potential; they activate it, stretch it, and turn it into performance.

This shift is not optional; it's essential. In fact, if you're not coaching, you're not really leading. You're simply overseeing tasks and people until something breaks. Leadership without coaching becomes supervision, and in today's fast-moving world, supervision alone will never be enough.

Coaching must become your daily rhythm. It should be embedded in your conversations, your one-on-ones, your goal-setting, and your culture. It's not a bonus for high-performers, it's the foundation for building a high-performing team. When you embrace this mindset, you stop asking, "How do I get more out of my people?" You start asking, "How do I grow what's already inside them?"

THE DEATH OF THE ANNUAL REVIEW
(And the Rise of Real-Time Growth)

Now, hear me out: Bruce Wayne.

Yeah, I know, but just stay with me.

Forget the billionaire playboy part for a second. I'm talking about the *obsessive, calculated, justice-driven* Bruce Wayne from The Dark Knight trilogy. The man didn't wing it, he didn't run on vibes, and he certainly didn't show up once a year to stop crime, give Gotham a "report," then dip back into the shadows.

Bruce was always watching, always learning, and always coaching himself in real-time. He studied the patterns of the city. He tracked criminals, anticipated chaos, upgraded his tactics, and reviewed every mission after the fact-immediately. If he got bruised in battle, he didn't wait until December to reflect. He'd go straight back to the Batcave, analyze footage, recalibrate his suit, and come back stronger the next night. Now, imagine if Batman operated the way most companies still do:

One review, once a year, generic feedback. "Good job, Bruce. Let's aim to reduce bruises by Q4."

Come on.

The annual review may have had a purpose back in 1967 when careers were linear, offices were centralized, and feedback was a one-way street. Back when your boss sat 10 feet from you, and your job looked exactly the same for the next 15 years. Back when innovation moved slower than molasses and leadership mostly meant keeping the ship from sinking.

But that world is gone.

Today, teams are global. Start-ups are scaling in months, industries are disrupted overnight, roles evolve faster than job descriptions can keep up, and your best people aren't waiting around twelve months to know how they're doing. If you're still relying on annual performance reviews as your primary tool for feedback and growth, you're not leading, you're sleepwalking.

Actually, most annual reviews don't develop anyone, they're bloated HR rituals. They're checkbox exercises, and they're feedback on things people forgot they even did. Worse, they create anxiety. That "big conversation" becomes a pressure cooker. Employees don't know what's coming, and even leaders scramble to remember details from 10 months ago. Everyone's pretending to be reflective, but really, they're just trying to survive the awkwardness. Don't get me started on the forced performance ratings that pit teammates against each other like it's *The Hunger Games*.

And all of that in a world where we now have the tools to do better. You've got Slack, notebooks, Zoom, email, Notion, AI, performance dashboards, daily check-ins, weekly one-on-ones, and many more. You've got all the data in the world, and yet... you're telling me your feedback cadence is still once a year?

If Bruce Wayne could analyze mission footage in a dark cave under his mansion, you can give your team better feedback than "keep up the good work" in December. Real leaders today build systems of continuous feedback. They treat growth like a rhythm, not a once-a-year surprise. They coach during the game, not after the season. They use tech to stay connected, to stay informed, to stay in the loop, and most importantly, they talk to their people. Not just about performance, but about direction, motivation, roadblocks, and goals. Regularly.

That's how transformation happens, not in a 50-minute recap of the year but in the small, honest, human moments-week by week, moment by moment.

So yes, the annual review had its run and maybe it served its purpose in the industrial age, but if you're still clinging to it in a fast-moving, human-first, digital world, you're not Batman, you're the commissioner filling out paperwork while Gotham burns.

BUILDING FEEDBACK INTO YOUR CULTURE

Most workplaces say they value feedback, but in practice, it's more like an awkward ritual. Something done once a year, with the energy of a dental appointment. Everyone braces, scripts are followed, politeness replaces truth and growth is optional.

However, world-class teams don't operate like that. They've moved feedback from something passive and periodic to something active and alive, not paperwork, but pulsework. It's not an event, it's a rhythm, and it's part of the culture's heartbeat.

Let me paint you a picture: Imagine a marching band; rigid, structured, predictable. Everything follows a script. Now compare that to a jazz band, fluid, responsive, alive in the moment. Jazz musicians aren't waiting for a quarterly note correction, they're constantly reading the room, adjusting to each other, and feeding off real-time cues. That's the shift we're talking about. From managing via forms and folders to leading via flow, and to do that, feedback has to become something leaders live, not just deliver.

Here's how you start building that feedback rhythm:

1. Set Your Coaching Cadence

Not all teams need the *same* beat, but they still all need *a* beat. Think of coaching cadences like heart rates; they vary by context, but without one, you flatline.

- For junior teams or new hires, weekly check-ins are oxygen.
- For mature, independent teams, biweekly or monthly sessions can work, provided they're deep, honest, and consistent.
- Don't wait until things break to start coaching. Great leaders stay ahead of the problem.

Make the time sacred and protect it because whatever you don't schedule gets swallowed by "urgent" chaos.

2. Use Simple Tools, Not Excuses

Technology has killed every excuse for disconnection. You can be across the world and still coach daily if you want to. Slack, Zoom, Loom, Google Docs—pick your flavor. The medium is secondary. What matters is presence.

Even an Async voice note that says, "Hey, I noticed how you handled that last client objection, solid control of tone and timing. Let's unpack it next time." That's gold and that's leadership. That's growth in motion.

3. Weave Feedback Into Your Rituals

You don't always need a 45-minute sit-down to coach. The best leaders embed growth moments into existing rhythms:

- Team meetings
- After action reviews: Quick debriefs after projects or sprints
- 1-minute nudges: Instant micro-feedback in real time
- Retro Fridays: Weekly rewind and reflections

The idea is this: don't isolate feedback; integrate it. It should flow so naturally that your team can't tell where coaching ends and collaboration begins.

4. Create Psychological Safety

None of this matters if your team doesn't feel safe to hear the truth or tell it. Feedback flows best in environments where people aren't punished for missteps but encouraged to learn from them. That means:

- Modeling vulnerability yourself
- Inviting pushback ("What am I missing?")
- Praising progress, not just perfection
- Making it normal to talk about what's *not* working

The more your team feels seen and safe, the more coachable they become, and the more coachable they are, the faster they grow.

5. Don't Just Call People Out, Call Them Up

Too many leaders use feedback as a weapon. "You screwed up, you didn't deliver." That's not coaching, that's critique. Great coaches don't just point at the gap, they build the bridge.

- Instead of "You messed up the handoff," try: "I think this could've gone smoother. How do you think we can tighten that next time?"
- Instead of "You're too quiet in meetings," try: "Your insights are strong. What's one way we can help you bring them into the room more often?"

Language shapes culture. Your words either shrink people or summon their next level. Be the kind of leader who speaks to someone's potential, not just their performance.

6. Feedback Must Flow *Upward*, Too

Last one—and it might be the hardest. If you want a coaching culture, you have to *be* coachable. Invite real feedback from your team. Make it safe to challenge your blind spots because leadership is a mirror, not a pedestal.

The moment your people stop telling you the truth is the moment you stop growing. If you stop growing, you can't lead anyone else forward.

The bottom line is that you can't outsource development, and you certainly can't automate growth. If you're serious about transformation, feedback has to go from once-a-year paperwork to a real-time pulse. Also, you-the leader-must be the heartbeat that sets the rhythm.

So, what do you say? Are you ready to stop managing reviews and start building revolutions? The choice is yours.

THE COACHING MINDSET

So, you've got your cadence. You've killed the outdated review model. You're feeding feedback into your rhythms. Now, let's pause for a second because tools are nothing without the mindset. You can have all the 1-on-1s on your calendar and even roll out fancy performance dashboards, but if your heart posture is off and your mentality is still rooted in ego, laziness, or emotional fragility, your coaching will collapse under the weight of your own baggage.

Coaching Requires Courage, Not Comfort

Let's call it what it is: Most people avoid feedback conversations because they're scared. Not because they're bad leaders or don't care, but because deep down, they fear conflict, rejection, or making someone cry at 10 a.m. on a Tuesday.

But leadership isn't a comfort game, it's a courage game. If you're choosing comfort over candor, you're not coaching, you're coddling. Real coaching demands the courage to speak the truth, even when it's awkward. The courage to confront lazy behavior without sugarcoating. The courage to push people past their excuses, even if it makes you unpopular for a while.

Leadership is hard, feedback is messy, and growth is uncomfortable, but if you're not willing to lean into that discomfort, you're not leading, you're hiding.

People Want to Grow, They're Just Not Used to Being Challenged

Most people secretly crave a challenge. They want to grow, but they just don't trust the system delivering the feedback because most of their experiences with feedback have been shady, vague, or weaponized. They've been criticized without clarity, judged without being developed, and told to "step up" with zero guidance on how.

Your job is to break that cycle. You're not here to be liked, but you're here to call people up to see in them what they can't yet see in themselves, and hold them to that standard with relentless belief. Not empty positivity or surface-level encouragement, but belief backed by accountability. You don't just say, "You can do better," rather you say, "I *know* you can do better, and I won't let you settle. Let's get it done."

It's Not Just About Hard Conversations, It's About Real Conversations

There's a crucial difference: Hard conversations are often forced, whereas real conversations are honest. You don't need to turn every coaching moment into a courtroom drama, you just need to be real, direct, and human.

Say things like:

"You've been showing up late consistently. That's not like you, so what's going on?"

"That last handoff was sloppy. Help me understand, what did you see that I didn't?"

"You've been coasting lately. Talk to me, what's behind it?"

It's not about confrontation, it's about connection. Real conversations build trust, and trust is what makes growth possible.

If You're Not Growing, You Can't Lead Growth

You can't coach from a stagnant place. If you're not being challenged, mentored, and refined, your coaching will lose weight. It'll become hollow—just recycled quotes and outdated advice on repeat, and trust me, people feel that. They smell it a mile away.

If you want to coach better, grow deeper; read more, get your own coach. And take feedback seriously because the truth is, your level of hunger, honesty, and humility sets the ceiling for your whole team.

Stop Taking Things So Personally

One of the biggest blockers in coaching is when leaders make everything about themselves.

"They didn't take my feedback well, maybe I said it wrong."

"They're underperforming, maybe I'm a bad leader."

"They pushed back, maybe they don't respect me."

News flash, it's not about you. People resist feedback for all kinds of reasons, for instance, fear, insecurity, distraction, or silent battles you'll never see. Your job isn't to take it personally but to stay consistent. Speak truth with love and stay rooted in respect, but don't get thrown off by every reaction. Coaching isn't about being liked, it's about building something that lasts and that means sometimes being misunderstood in the moment so that someone can transform down the line.

Hold the Standard Even When It Hurts

Let's be blunt: if you don't hold the line, you're lowering the bar...

You can't claim to coach people toward greatness while tolerating mediocrity. You can't keep preaching "high-performance culture" while rewarding low-effort, high-drama energy. Your silence becomes your endorsement. I have a principle that silence means consent, so I'm skeptical about when I remain silent and when I can't let it slide. That's the weight of leadership. The moment you look away from the standard, you start teaching people that average is acceptable. And yes, it'll hurt. You'll have days where you feel like the bad guy, but have it at the back of your mind that you're not the villain, you're the guardian of the standard. One day, they'll thank you, not always with words, but with growth.

Consistency > Intensity

Anyone can have a great day, but leaders aren't measured by what they do occasionally; they're measured by what they do repeatedly. The temptation is to celebrate flashes of brilliance; the all-nighters, the emotional pep talks, the dramatic turnarounds, whereas real impact doesn't come from intensity, it comes from consistency.

Intensity is loud and impressive in the moment, but it's short-lived. Consistency is quieter, but it compounds. Over time, it builds trust, shapes culture, and sets the pace for the entire team. As a coach, your job isn't to spark occasional hype, it's to create systems and rhythms that sustain excellence. You need to show up when it's boring, coach when it's inconvenient, and stay anchored when the energy dips and the motivation wears off.

Your team doesn't need you to be explosive, they need you to be dependable because, in the end, the leaders who win aren't the ones who burn the brightest for a moment but the ones who burn steadily-day after day, long enough to light the way for others.

Coaching the Quiet Performers

Not every top performer is loud, and not every future leader is the one constantly raising their hand. Some of your strongest team members are the quiet ones, steady, consistent, and often under-celebrated. They don't chase attention or self-promote, but they show up every day and deliver with quiet excellence.

The real danger is that they often get overlooked. They receive less feedback, less coaching, and fewer opportunities and not because they lack potential, but because they don't demand visibility. Their silence becomes their invisibility.

As a leader, it's your responsibility to see them, to notice what others miss. Leadership isn't about rewarding noise, it's about recognizing value. Don't just coach the squeaky wheels, develop the silent engines that keep things moving when no one's watching. Make space for their voice. Invite them into deeper conversations and say things like, "I've noticed how consistent and composed you've been lately, let's talk about what growth looks like for you," or "The way you handle pressure is impressive, have you considered mentoring others?"

Sometimes, the quietest person in the room is carrying the loudest potential. All they need is a leader with the eyes to see it and the courage to call it out and coach the hell out of them. Be that leader.

In a nutshell, coaching is a sacred trust, not a strategy. It's not some clever leadership trick or a checkbox to tick during quarterly reviews. It is a sacred responsibility—a high-stakes commitment to developing the potential buried inside another human being. When you step into the role of a coach, you are doing more than giving feedback or setting goals, you are shaping lives and pulling greatness out of people who may have stopped believing it exists. You are demanding excellence in a world that's addicted to comfort. You are, quite literally, raising the standard, one conversation at a time.

This work is not for the lazy or the insecure, and it's definitely not for the leader who just wants peace and quiet. It's for the bold, the present, the persistent, because if you get this right, you won't just see better performance, you'll create people who lead themselves long after you're gone, and that's legacy.

THE COACHING PLAYBOOK

You don't become a great coach by accident; you become one on purpose, through rhythm, repetition, and ruthless intention. The best leaders don't just inspire, they equip. They know when to speak, when to stay silent, when to challenge, and when to let people wrestle with the weight themselves.

If you want transformation, not just performance, you need a playbook. Let's break down the most powerful coaching styles every modern leader should master.

1. Spot Coaching

Think of spot coaching like in-game adjustments. The play is happening, the clock is ticking, and there's no time for a Zoom meeting or performance review. You see a blind spot, a gap, a behavior that's off or on point, and you respond immediately. This kind of coaching is fast, agile, and surgical. But it only works if:

- You're paying attention (coaches who don't watch the game miss everything).
- You have relational capital, so people don't feel ambushed or humiliated.
- You know how to give tight, clear, and actionable feedback in less than 60 seconds.

Example:

"Hey, I noticed in that client pitch you kept interrupting her. You're coming in strong, but you're not letting the buyer process. Pull back 20%. Trust your silence, it sells more than your words."

That's coaching in real time. Real sharp, no fluff.

2. Pattern Coaching

People repeat both good and bad patterns, and so your job, then, is to spot the loops that are either accelerating someone's growth or sabotaging it. Pattern coaching requires tracking over time, not just reacting in the moment. It's when you start to say, "I've noticed you tend to get defensive when your ideas are challenged," or "Every time pressure hits, you go dark instead of reaching out." You're not correcting a single moment, you're confronting a habit.

Done right, pattern coaching feels like holding up a mirror:

"I want to show you something I've been seeing consistently. I'm not attacking you, I'm trying to unlock you."

Most people have no idea how their own loops are limiting them. Great leaders help them see it without shame.

3. Growth Coaching

This is the long game. It's not about what they did this week, it's about where they could be six months from now.

Growth coaching requires:

- Stretch assignments tied to development goals
- Skill ladders, not vague aspirations like "get better at communication"
- Honest questions like: "What kind of leader do you want to be?", "What's in your way?", and "What's a real win for you, not just for the company?"

This is where the real magic happens. It turns employees into vision-driven contributors. It shifts their identity from "task doer" to "builder, owner, future leader," and when someone sees you've got a plan for them, not just from them, loyalty deepens.

4. Crisis Coaching

Ultimately, everyone hits walls, everyone fails, and everyone breaks. How you show up in those moments defines your culture more than any value on your website.

Crisis coaching is less about strategy and more about presence.

- You sit in the mess with them
- You don't sugarcoat or over-rescue

- You say things like: "This is hard, but it doesn't have to define you."

"Let's find the lesson before we move on."

Real leaders don't just celebrate wins; they walk people through their losses and teach them how to lose well so they bounce back stronger.

Practical Tools for Every Coaching Style

Let's land this with tools you can use in any style:

- **The 3 As Framework**: Awareness, Adjustment, Accountability. Every coaching moment should hit at least two of these.
- **Use more questions than answers**: Try "What do you think is driving that?" before telling them what's wrong.
- **Track growth in public**: Use shared notes or dashboards to show progress over time. Nothing inspires like visible momentum.
- **Build rituals**: Maybe every Friday, you send one coaching reflection to your direct reports. Keep it light, but intentional.

Great coaches don't wait for people to crash. They see the drift before it becomes a disaster. They water potential before it turns into frustration. They speak identity into people when all they see is inadequacy, and when it's time to challenge someone, they don't hesitate because they've earned the right to be heard.

So, do you want transformation? Well, don't just lead people, coach them like you mean it. In a world where talent has options, people won't stick around for managers who just assign tasks and check boxes. They want leaders who see them, stretch them, and believe in who they can become, not just what they can produce.

Feedback

Yes, we already talked about feedback when we unpacked coaching, but this deserves its own spotlight because feedback is where most leaders fail, honestly. They either sugarcoat it until it's meaningless, or they drop truth bombs with zero emotional intelligence and wonder why their team ghosts them. Either way, they lose.

If your feedback doesn't land, nothing else matters. Not your vision, not your strategy, and not your "open door" policy because people don't grow from silence, and they sure as hell don't grow from shame. What follows is how you give feedback that actually

helps people level up without sparking resentment, defensiveness, or quiet quitting.

1. First, Fix the Mindset

If you believe feedback is about criticism, you'll weaponize it. If you believe it's about correction, you'll sound like a parent. But if you believe it's about alignment and growth, you'll lead like a coach. The best leaders don't give feedback to feel superior, they give it to create clarity about standards, behavior, expectations, and potential.

Feedback is the mirror that helps your team see what they can't see on their own. If you withhold it, you're not being kind, you're being selfish because silence keeps them stuck. So, ask yourself this: "Do I care more about their comfort or their growth?"

2. Use a Framework — Don't Freestyle the Truth

Winging feedback is leadership malpractice. When you shoot from the hip, two things usually happen: you speak from emotion, and they hear from defense. The result is always either confusion, hurt, resentment, or, worst of all, no change.

Great leaders don't freestyle truth, they deliver it with precision. That's why the best in the game use structured frameworks to ground their feedback in observable behavior, not assumptions; in care, not control.

Here are two that have stood the test of battle in real organizations, from start-ups to Fortune 500s:

Radical Candor

This framework was pioneered by Kim Scott, a former executive at Google and Apple who spent years studying what makes feedback land without destroying relationships. Her insight was simple but powerful: feedback that fuels growth sits at the intersection of caring personally and challenging directly (*Radical Candor Framework*, n.d.). It's a quadrant model with four zones:

Style	Care Personally	Challenge Directly	Outcome
Radical Candor	High	High	Growth, trust, accountability
Ruinous Empathy	High	Low	Comfort, but stagnation
Obnoxious Aggression	High	High	Fear, resentment
Manipulative Insincerity	Low	Low	Politics, dysfunction

Radical Candor is what you want, especially when you intend to tell the hard truth but from a place of care. You're not trying to crush someone's spirit, you're trying to unlock their next level. For instance, you can say something like: "You're capable of so much more, and I'd be doing you a disservice if I didn't point this out." That's radically candid and also honest, but it's also anchored in belief and respect. What you want to avoid:

- Ruinous Empathy: "It's okay, no worries, let's just keep things as is."
- You mean well, but you're enabling mediocrity.
- Obnoxious Aggression: "Why do you always screw this up?"
- You might be right, but now they're hurt and checked out.
- Manipulative Insincerity: "This is fine" (but you secretly vent about it later).
- This erodes trust, and they always find out.

Radical Candor strikes the rare balance—it's not soft or savage, just clear, human, and direct.

SBI: Situation – Behavior – Impact

The SBI model was developed by the Center for Creative Leadership, one of the top leadership institutions in the world. It's built on the principle that people can't grow from vague feedback; they grow from concrete moments and clear effects (Center for Creative Leadership, 2022). The structure is simple, but surgical:

- Situation – Describe when and where it happened > "Yesterday in the client meeting…"
- Behavior – Describe exactly what the person did > "…you interrupted the client several times…"
- Impact – Describe how it affected others, the work, or the outcome > "…which made them feel dismissed and frustrated. We risk losing trust."

This works very well because it's objective, not emotional. It focuses on the behavior, not the person. Also, it links the action to its real-world consequences. Furthermore, with SBI, you replace accusations with clarity, which opens the door to growth because the person understands exactly what happened, why it matters, and what needs to change.

So, neither of these frameworks is magic; they won't make hard conversations easy, but they make them effective. They remove the drama, turn feedback from personal attacks into professional development, and they help you speak hard truths without losing the room. The best leaders don't just say what needs to be said; they say it in a way that can be heard. That's the difference between unloading feedback and unlocking someone's future. Let's identify the differences practically:

Scenario	Poor Feedback	Strong Feedback (Radical Candor / SBI)	Why It Works
Missed Deadline	"Why are you always late? This is becoming a habit."	"On Monday's deadline (Situation), you submitted late (Behavior), which delayed the client handoff (Impact). Let's discuss how to prevent this."	Specific, not emotional. Solution-oriented.
Negative Attitude	"Be more of a team player. Everyone notices."	"I've noticed eye-rolling in meetings. Your presence matters. It's affecting morale, and I know you can improve."	Clear, caring, and honest. Tackles behavior, not character.
Mediocre Work	"It's fine, I know you're busy."	"You're sharp, which is why the gaps surprised me. Take another pass, I know you can do better."	Holds a high bar with belief. Promotes growth.
Chronic Lateness	"You're late again. This is getting ridiculous."	"Over two weeks (Situation), you were late three times (Behavior), disrupting flow (Impact). Let's talk about what's happening."	Facts > Frustration. Invites dialogue.
Overstepping Boundaries	"Next time, maybe loop us in first?"	"At Friday's demo (Situation), you announced unapproved features (Behavior), which confused the client (Impact). I value your drive, so let's align next time."	Balanced correction with affirmation. Maintains trust.

So, the tables gave you contrast, now here's the code: The Justice League had their motto, athletes have their playbook, military teams live by standard operating procedures, but high-performing leaders; they live and die by 'The Ten Commandments of Feedback (Gottlleb, 2023).' This is the gospel for any leader who wants to grow people without breaking them.

- Thou shalt not wing it.
  - o If you can't say it with clarity, don't say it yet. Prepare, ground yourself in facts.
- Thou shalt speak to the behavior, not the person.
  - o "You dropped the ball on the report" to "You're unreliable." One invites change, the other attacks identity.
- Thou shalt care deeply and challenge directly.
  - o Be human, but don't coddle. Growth requires tension and trust.
- Thou shalt be specific.
  - o Great job is lazy. "The way you reframed the objection in that sales call is brilliant" is gold.
- Thou shalt give feedback often, not just when it's broken.
  - o Annual reviews are cemeteries, frequent feedback is oxygen.
- Thou shalt ask, not assume.
  - o Don't diagnose before you listen. "Help me understand what happened there..." goes further than blame.
- Thou shalt calibrate your tone.
  - o Your words matter, but so does your delivery. Say hard things softly, but clearly.

- Thou shalt follow up.
  - o Feedback without follow-up is just a speech, growth is proven in progress.
- Thou shalt normalize feedback.
  - o Don't make it a big, scary moment; make it part of your leadership rhythm.
- Thou shalt never forget: feedback is a gift.
  - o But only if it's wrapped in clarity, humility, and a genuine desire to help them grow.

Making Feedback the Culture

Pixar Animation Studios isn't just known for its storytelling; it's known for how it tells the truth within the company. At the heart of its success is a feedback culture called "The Braintrust."

The Braintrust is a recurring meeting where directors present rough versions of their films to a group of trusted peers. There's one rule: candor above comfort. No sugarcoating or ego-stroking, just clear, constructive feedback from people who care deeply about the work and the people behind it. What makes it powerful is:

- No Hierarchy – A junior storyboard artist can challenge a director.
- No Fear – The culture makes it safe to speak up.
- No Blame – Feedback is about the work, not the person.

Brad Bird, the director of *The Incredibles*, once said the Braintrust saved the movie. The early cuts didn't land. It was honest, brutal feedback delivered with respect that helped him reshape the story into a global hit. That's what feedback culture looks like. It's not a meeting but a mindset, and when done right, it doesn't just improve performance, it fuels excellence.

COACHING LEADERS OF TOMORROW

Okay, so we've spent time on feedback—not just on how to deliver it, but on how to normalize it. We've explored what it means to create a culture where people grow through truth, not flattery. Now, feedback is not just a tool for fixing performance, it's a system for identifying and shaping the leaders of tomorrow. That brings us to the next crucial conversation.

It's clearer now what happens when leaders fail to prepare their successors. The consequences aren't abstract, they're visible. Kingdoms fall, empires crumble, and organizations get infiltrated, disrupted, and eventually outpaced. There's no need to repeat the warning.

The real question isn't "what happens if we don't prepare future leaders?" The real question is: how do we identify the people who are ready?

Who can handle responsibility without losing perspective?

Who's hungry for growth, not just attention?

Who carries weight quietly, long before they're handed a title?

A premature promotion doesn't just slow things down, it drains momentum, breeds entitlement, and sends a message to the rest of the team that political moves matter more than performance and character. So instead of playing favorites or guessing based on tenure, we need a better approach.

The truth is that promotions are not rewards, they're bets. High-stakes bets actually and the leaders who confuse loyalty for leadership or tenure for potential often end up crippling their teams with the wrong people in elevated roles. Just because someone has stuck around through the storm doesn't mean they should be handed the wheel. Just because they can execute well under instructions doesn't mean they can think, lead, and multiply under pressure. We've all seen it: the top salesperson promoted to manager, only to lose their edge while failing to elevate anyone else. The veteran employee who's been around for years gets handed a bigger title out of convenience, only to drag culture down with apathy and low standards. Promotions done wrong are more damaging than no promotions at all.

So, what exactly should we look for when spotting true promotable talent?

First, look for ownership. People who take initiative without needing to be pushed. They don't just perform tasks, they take responsibility for outcomes. They think like owners even if they hold no equity. When things go wrong, they don't look for someone to blame or wait for rescue, they get up and fix it. Quietly and consistently.

Second, emotional maturity. At higher levels, pressure doesn't decrease; it multiplies. If someone melts under feedback, personalizes tension, or avoids difficult conversations, they're not ready. The higher the position, the greater the emotional resilience required.

Third, look for multiplication energy. Do people naturally follow them? Do they lift others up without being asked to? Do they spread knowledge, energy, and excellence just by how they show up? Promotable people don't compete with their peers, they elevate them. They make others better by proximity.

And finally, don't ignore pattern recognition. At the highest levels, leadership becomes less about execution and more about perception. Do they see blind spots? Can they predict outcomes before they happen? Do they move with strategic clarity or react impulsively to what's in front of them?

The 4 Cs of Promotable Talent

1. **Character** – Do they do the right thing when nobody's watching? Can they be trusted with power without letting it corrupt their judgment?

2. **Competence** – Not just can they execute, but can they think critically, solve problems, and grow into strategic challenges?

3. **Capacity** – Do they have the bandwidth—mentally, emotionally, and logistically—to handle more? Can they stretch without snapping?

4. **Contribution** – Are they already adding value beyond their role? Are they lifting others, building culture, and driving results without needing a title?

If you've got someone with initiative, maturity, multiplication, and vision, you don't just have a top performer, you have someone worth building around. Without that, all you're doing is inflating titles and adding layers of frustration.

Promoting Without Breaking the Culture

Promotions aren't just a change in title, they're a signal. They shape what your team believes about success, leadership, and what's truly valued. Promote the wrong person, and people stop aiming high. Promote the right one, and everyone levels up.

Done right, promoting from within is one of the most powerful growth strategies you have. It's cheaper than hiring externally. Research shows it can save around 20% per hire. More importantly, internal candidates already know the culture, the systems, the stakes. They've been in the trenches so they don't need onboarding, they need elevation.

Unfortunately, most leaders often treat promotions like rewards instead of responsibilities. Handing someone a new title because they've earned it through tenure or loyalty is lazy leadership, and it's not a promotion; that's a shortcut. It's one of the fastest ways to introduce entitlement and resentment into your culture. True promotions are a bet on future contribution, not a prize for past performance.

So, how do you promote well? Start by helping people design their own path. You don't have to play career counselor, but you do need to know what drives your team. What kind of work lights them up? What roles do they see themselves growing into? What challenges bring out their best? Too many leaders guess at this, or worse, assume everyone wants to move up. Some don't. Some want mastery, others want freedom, some want to lead people, and others want to build systems. Your job is to have the conversations that surface those desires and build growth paths that align both the company's needs and the person's design.

Don't force your best executor into management if they hate people. Don't bury a future leader in IC work if they're ready to scale others.

Once those paths are clear, create space for stretch assignments or projects that test leadership, expose decision-making, and reveal how someone handles weight. Observe them under pressure. Give real feedback, not just praise, then watch what they do with it.

And never promote in a vacuum. When someone steps into a new role, their influence shifts immediately. People take cues from who gets elevated. They adjust their own standards, behavior, and aspirations. So, before you promote, ask:

- What message will this send to the team?
- Is this person ready to multiply others, or will they manage from ego?
- Will this promotion raise the bar or reinforce the wrong behavior?

Always remember that the wrong promotion can't just be undone quietly—it leaves a dent on culture, trust, and momentum The right promotion, though, energizes the room and tells people, "This is what we value. This is what we reward, and this is what you can grow into."

FOOTPRINTS OF A LEADER

Great leaders build people. They take the time to notice and study the efforts of everyone and then they invest or reward accordingly. Why? Because leadership is about legacy; It's the invisible fingerprints you leave on people who go on to lead without you.

Let me tell you a story.

When I joined a fully remote online company as COO, I inherited a globally distributed team comprising time zones, cultures, and communication styles, all over the map. One of those team members was a quiet, entry-level contributor based in Africa. Let's call him Robert.

Robert didn't come with credentials or a polished leadership résumé. However, what he had was hunger. He showed up with questions and chased feedback. He wanted to grow—he just needed someone to show him how.

So I did.

Every week, without fail, we met for an hour. We didn't just review performance, we talked about leadership and walked through hard scenarios together. I gave him tough assignments that would test his thinking, challenge his emotional maturity, and stretch his influence.

He took it seriously, and within a year, Robert had been promoted twice and was leading an entire department. Not because of politics or seniority, but because of preparation. He mirrored everything we worked on and poured it back into his team. He was coaching others before he even had the title to do it.

To this day, he still checks in. Still grateful. Still growing and what sticks with me most is something someone once said after hearing his story: "You've got your footprints all over him."

This is the work of coaching and growth. It's not glamorous, but it's legacy work that turns high performers into high-capacity leaders. The kind that leaves a trail others can follow.

If you're wondering how to begin, let's break it down step by step.

Here's your Monday Morning Playbook:

MONDAY MORNING
PLAYBOOK

Great teams aren't managed, they're developed. If you're not coaching your people, you're not leading them. Growth doesn't happen by accident, it happens because you demand it.

🧠 MINDSET SHIFT:

If your team only hears feedback once a year, you're not their coach, you're a stranger. People don't grow in silence, they grow from consistency, challenge, and clarity.

✓ DO THIS MONDAY:

1. Lock In Weekly 1-on-1s (By End of Day Today)

- Book 30 minutes with each direct report. No exceptions.
- If it's not on your calendar by the end of today, it doesn't exist.
- Use the same agenda every time: What's going well and what's stuck?

2. Ask One Person What They Want to Improve (Today, Not Tomorrow)

- Not what you want, what they want. You're not a mind reader, you're a leader.
- Ask them, "What's one skill or area you want to get better at?" Then listen.
- Follow up with, "How can I support you in making that happen?"
- Growth is a partnership. If you're doing all the driving, they're just along for the ride.

3. Give One Piece of Constructive Feedback Today, Not Next Week

- Not when it's "easier." Not when you're "less busy." Today.
- Make it clear, specific, and direct. No sugar, no sandwich.
- Say this: "Here's what I saw. Here's why it matters. Here's how we make it better."
- Your job is to sharpen the blade, not dull it with politeness. If you're holding back feedback to "be nice," you're protecting feelings and sacrificing growth.

CHAPTER 6:

HARNESS THE FIRE – TURNING CONFLICT INTO CULTURE FUEL

"Peace is not the absence of conflict, but the ability to cope with it."
– Mahatma Gandhi

In the business world, especially in leadership, conflict isn't a glitch in the system. It is the system testing your integrity, maturity, and leadership backbone. If you're building anything worthwhile, involving a culture of excellence, high performance, and accountability, then brace yourself: conflict is coming. And not just once or occasionally, it will show up repeatedly, like an uninvited guest at the table of progress.

Some leaders flinch, others freeze, but the best embrace it, because they understand something most don't: conflict isn't the enemy, unresolved conflict is.

Too many managers and founders believe that great teams always get along or that a healthy culture means no tension. Even society often feeds us the lie that disagreements equal dysfunction. When there's never any disagreement, it usually means people don't feel safe enough to speak. Worse, it might mean they've stopped caring altogether.

Conflict is a pressure test for trust, maturity, and alignment to the mission. It reveals who's truly committed versus who's merely compliant. It exposes whether your culture runs on candor or convenience. Most importantly, it's where the real work of leadership begins.

How you handle conflict doesn't just affect how people feel; it shapes what your team becomes. Will your people learn to suppress their voices, or will they trust the system, knowing that tough conversations are welcome, respected, and resolved? That's on you. That's leadership.

Avoiding conflict is not an option; mastering it is a requirement. In fact, we need to go deeper. Let's unpack conflict thoroughly, from its different types to practical frameworks that help you handle it like a seasoned pro. We'll explore mediation tactics, how to spot toxic patterns early, and how to rebuild trust once the dust has settled.

Whether you're dealing with two teammates who can't work together, a passive-aggressive powder keg, or a personal clash threatening to fracture your culture, you'll walk away with the mindset, tools, and voice to boss it up like a true coach.

TYPES OF CONFLICT YOU'LL ENCOUNTER AS A LEADER

Not all conflict is created equal, some tensions are creative and necessary whereas others are corrosive and dangerous. The key to becoming a masterful leader isn't avoiding conflict, but learning to diagnose it properly before you try to address it. Conflict is like illness; if you misdiagnose it, you'll mistreat it and mistreated conflict doesn't heal, it metastasizes.

Let's break it down into three core types every leader will face:

Task-Based Conflict

Task-based conflict isn't personal, it's professional. It surfaces when people disagree on how something should be done, what the priorities should be, or who should take the lead on certain responsibilities (Pollack, n.d.). In its healthiest form, this kind of conflict is actually a sign that people care. They're engaged and thinking critically. It also shows that they're wrestling with the work because it matters to them.

Nonetheless, just because it's professional doesn't mean it's always pleasant. Task conflict, if mishandled, can spiral quickly into tension, frustration, and stalled progress. Think about two high-performers arguing passionately in a meeting: one believes in moving fast, testing ideas quickly, and iterating on the fly. The other is a perfectionist by nature; meticulous, process-driven, wanting every detail locked in before launch. The conversation starts with strategy, but by the 20-minute mark, it's become a power struggle. Voices rise, and others in the room go silent. What could have been a rich moment of ideation now feels like a cold war.

This is task-based conflict at a crossroads. It can either lead to clarity or chaos. Collaboration or cold shoulders.

What's often misunderstood is that task conflict doesn't indicate dysfunction; it's a natural byproduct of diversity, thought, experience, discipline, and working style. You want people who think differently. That's how you get to sharper ideas and smarter execution. The real problem isn't that there's disagreement but that most teams don't know how to handle disagreement well.

Instead of turning tension into traction, they avoid it. They default to politeness or they argue for argument's sake, digging in not because they're right, but because they hate being wrong. In both cases, the outcome is the same: the work suffers.

Now, here's where leadership becomes nonnegotiable.

A mature leader doesn't shut down disagreement, they structure it. They don't play referee in a war of egos; they act more like a conductor guiding the rhythm, setting the tempo, making sure the different instruments create music, not noise. That means stepping in without taking sides, then clarifying the problem and keeping the focus on the work, not the personalities.

It also means knowing when to let the team debate freely and when to bring closure. because there's a fine line between creative tension and circular debate. At some point, someone has to make a call and the team needs to trust that the decision will be made, even if not everyone agrees. That's leadership, and that's where decisiveness becomes oxygen for momentum.

Here's another key point: task conflict only works in environments with psychological safety; that's the real currency. Without it, people won't speak up, they'll withhold ideas to avoid tension, or worse, they'll say nothing in the room, and everything behind closed doors. You'll get fake harmony in public and real resentment in private, and that's deadly.

So, what does a healthy environment for task conflict look like?

- Team members challenging each other's ideas without attacking the person behind them.
- People feeling free to say "I disagree" without fearing backlash or labels.
- Leaders modeling curiosity over control, asking more than they dictate.
- Meetings that surface tension, not suppress it, and then resolve it with clarity and alignment.

When done right, task conflict becomes a form of sharpening. It's not an interruption to progress, it's progress. It's the fire where great strategy is forged, and weak ideas are refined or discarded. Without it, teams grow stale, echo chambers form, and execution suffers. You'll know you've mastered it when your team can go head-to-head on strategy at 10 a.m., and still grab lunch together at 12 because they know the battle is about the mission, not about each other.

So, the real question isn't: "How do I avoid conflict on my team?" The real question is: "Have I built a team and a culture that knows how to fight well?"

Relationship-Based Conflict

This is the kind of conflict that seeps deep into team culture. This one has nothing to do with missed deadlines or project disagreements. It's about people; who they are, how they operate, what they value, and, sometimes, unresolved emotional friction that simmers beneath the surface (Pollack, 2024).

You'll see it when two employees just don't get along. Maybe one's super direct while the other is sensitive and passive-aggressive, or one's always trying to lead everything, while the other just wants to contribute in peace. Often, it's a clash of personality, values, or even past unresolved tensions that never got addressed.

Unfortunately, relationship-based conflict doesn't stay contained; it leaks. It affects communication, slows collaboration, and poisons morale. Over time, it creates factions, people start choosing sides, withholding ideas, or working around each other instead of with each other.

It also forces leaders into difficult terrain. You're not just resolving a disagreement about strategy, you're helping grown adults manage emotions, perceptions, and pride, and if you're not careful, you end up playing therapist instead of leader.

Furthermore, unresolved relationship conflicts often masquerade as performance issues or communication breakdowns but if you dig deeper, what you'll find is two people with hurt feelings, resentment, or ego friction.

So, what do you do instead?

First, you don't ignore it. This kind of conflict never goes away on its own; the tension just builds and starts infecting the culture. Instead, you step in early. Don't let small relational conflicts metastasize into full-blown feuds. Ideally, you want to intercept it when it's still a minor irritation, not emotional warfare.

Start by having private 1-on-1 conversations with each party. Your goal here isn't to judge or pick sides but to understand how each person is experiencing the conflict and what's driving their frustration. Listen, take notes, and look for emotional clues. Sometimes what they're saying isn't the root; it's how they feel that holds the key.

Next, move to a facilitated conversation. This isn't some kumbaya circle, it's a structured conversation with rules. Set the tone: mutual respect, no interrupting, focus on facts and feelings, not blame. Let each person speak, then paraphrase what you hear to confirm understanding.

You can also ask key questions like:

- "What do you think they misunderstood about you?"
- "What do you think your role in the breakdown might have been?"
- "What would help restore working trust between you?"

You're not looking for best friends here, you're aiming for functional respect and alignment. The goal is professional peace, not personal closeness. Once the air is cleared, set mutual commitments moving forward. These are behavioral expectations that both parties agree to. Things like: "We'll keep each other informed of key updates," or "We'll bring concerns up directly, not through side conversations." Write these down, follow up, and hold them accountable. Make no mistake, though, if one person refuses to adjust, continues to stir tension, or undermines the commitments, it becomes a performance issue. At that point, you escalate accordingly.

Relationship conflict isn't always 50/50, sometimes, one person is just consistently antagonistic or toxic. Don't let a neutral posture prevent you from making hard calls when one side clearly won't grow or change.

Leadership-Based Conflict

Some of the most frustrating and difficult conflicts you'll ever face as a leader are the ones where you are the source. Not intentionally or maliciously, but it happens because leadership isn't neutral. Every decision, tone, priority, or lack thereof, creates ripple effects and sometimes, those ripples turn into waves that crash into your own team.

Now, leadership-based conflict doesn't always look like shouting matches or dramatic walkouts. In fact, it's often quieter and harder to detect at first. You'll notice it in missed deadlines, cold silences in meetings, a team that seems to say "yes" but acts out "no." It shows up in subtle defiance, withheld effort, or even polite distance. When that happens, it's time to stop pointing outward and start asking hard questions inward.

Most of the time, this conflict stems from a mismatch. A mismatch between what you think you're communicating and what your team is hearing, a mismatch between how you perceive your leadership and how they experience it, or a mismatch between your intent and your impact. Sadly, many leaders unknowingly create the very dysfunction they later try to fix.

Conflict, when handled right, is feedback. It's a sign that something needs attention, whether that's your approach, their perception, or both. In fact, if people trust you enough to disagree to your face, you're doing something right. It means there's at least some degree of psychological safety. Now, if they're only venting behind closed doors, walking on eggshells around you, or nodding in silence while privately tuning you out, then that's a leadership crisis waiting to unfold.

Let me show you what this looks like in real life.

A few years back, I was coaching a start-up founder who had scaled quickly. Within a year, he went from five employees to over fifty. But something started breaking. Turnover increased, and his leadership team seemed disengaged. He couldn't get people to take ownership. "They're lazy," he said. "They don't care like I do."

So, I did some digging.

What I discovered was this: the issue wasn't laziness, it was confusion and fear. The founder was constantly shifting priorities, micromanaging tiny decisions, and blowing up in frustration when things weren't perfect. His team had no clue what the actual North Star was. People felt belittled, second-guessed, and exhausted.

I pulled him aside and said, "You're not leading a team. You're playing whack-a-mole with people's confidence."

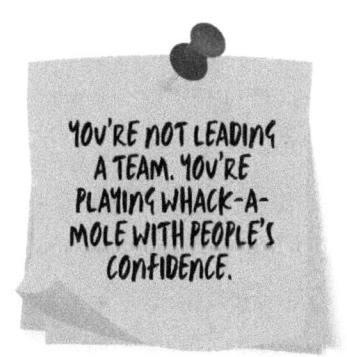

It hit hard but to his credit, he didn't get defensive. He sat down with each of his senior leaders and asked the uncomfortable questions. He owned his part then he restructured the organization to clarify expectations, delegated real authority, and committed to weekly feedback loops. Within three months, the culture began to shift. Not because the people changed, but because the leader changed.

So, what can you take from that?

Before you react to conflict with disappointment or blame, do a self-check. Ask: *Have I been clear? Have I been consistent? Have I made people feel safe to tell me the truth even when it hurts?*

Remember, the best leaders aren't the ones who avoid conflict; they're the ones who know how to recognize it early, embrace it humbly, and resolve it honorably.

Sometimes, that means apologizing while other times, it means resetting expectations. And sometimes it can even mean letting go of someone who refuses to be led, no matter how much you adjust. But the goal is always the same: alignment, trust, and growth on both sides.

Value-Based Conflict

Most conflicts in teams don't start with a missed deadline or a sloppy presentation—those are just surface ripples. The deeper rifts come from values. The kind of conflict that doesn't go away with a quick apology or a Monday morning reset meeting. This is the stuff that simmers under the skin, for instance, two people who fundamentally view the world, the mission, or what good work looks like in opposite ways. That's value-based conflict.

And it's dangerous, not because people have different values—I mean, that part is normal—but because most leaders don't know how to handle it when it surfaces.

Value-based conflict arises when people are guided by different internal compasses. It's not just a disagreement about what is being done, it's about why it's being done, how it should be done, and what truly matters. These conflicts often surface through debates over priorities, work ethic, communication styles, or leadership philosophies. But beneath the surface, it's not really about the task at hand, it's about values—what someone deeply believes is right, important, or non-negotiable (Rose, 2020).

Let's say you have someone on your team who deeply values speed and believes "done is better than perfect." Meanwhile, their teammate values excellence and refuses to ship anything that doesn't meet their standard. On the surface, they're arguing about a launch deadline, but under the hood, it's a war of values. One sees the delay as a failure, whereas the other sees speed as a compromise. See the clash?

Here's another: One employee believes in brutal honesty and calls things out in real-time. Their teammate believes in diplomacy and emotional intelligence. Suddenly, a casual feedback conversation turns into a cold war. Why? Values. They're not speaking the same language.

Now, one might wonder, is this a bad thing? Well, not necessarily. Value-based conflict isn't always toxic. In fact, when handled well, it can *sharpen* a team and deepen mutual respect, but then when ignored or handled poorly, it can fracture trust, sabotage collaboration, and infect culture. That's why mature leaders must learn to recognize this type of conflict early and lean in, not pull back.

You can't "policy" your way out of value-based conflict. This doesn't just require SOPs anymore, It requires awareness, coaching, and courageous leadership.

There is this founder that I coached recently. Let's call him Jason. Brilliant guy, built a SaaS company from scratch. One of his key department heads, Amanda, was just as sharp, operationally excellent, process-driven, and a total machine. However, they kept clashing repeatedly, and not over performance. I mean, Amanda was delivering. The issue was that Jason was deeply mission-driven. Every decision he made was tied to the *why*, while Amanda was all about the *how*, the efficiency, and the results.

Their 1:1s kept ending in frustration. Jason felt Amanda didn't get it. Amanda felt Jason was wasting time with emotional noise. On paper, both were right, but then they were locked in a value-based conflict. I had to help Jason see that Amanda wasn't rebellious; she was just rooted in different soil. The fix wasn't firing her, it was about finding alignment, realigning expectations, clarifying nonnegotiables, and building mutual respect around those differences. Once Jason stopped trying to convert Amanda into a "mini-him," things shifted. They actually started to complement each other, but only after facing the value clash head-on.

So, as a leader, the first step is to "*Name it.*" Most leaders react to the behavior, not the *belief* driving it. "Why does she always push back?" "Why is he so passive-aggressive?" Wrong questions; you have to ask: "What value is being challenged here?"

Next, create space for conversations about values. This is why onboarding is critical and also why team norms matter. When values are made explicit, it gives people a language to talk about the tension before it becomes resentment.

Then, coach. Sometimes one value needs to stretch to meet another. Sometimes you realize someone's core values are out of sync with the company's, and that's a different conversation altogether. Nonetheless, that clarity is gold.

Personality Clashes

Let's be honest; some people just rub you the wrong way, and sometimes you rub people the wrong way too. That doesn't make either of you villains, it just means your operating systems are clashing. Personality clashes aren't necessarily the result of hurt feelings or unresolved drama, no, this is deeper or perhaps simpler. It's about temperament, communication style, and wiring.

For instance:

- The high-energy extrovert who thrives on spontaneous brainstorms vs. the deep-thinking introvert who needs time and quiet to reflect.
- The blunt "just tell me straight" type vs. the diplomatic "let's not offend anyone" peacemaker.
- The optimist who sees every problem as a challenge versus the realist who's constantly warning about risks.

On paper, they might all be excellent at their jobs, but put them on the same team without awareness or adaptability, and suddenly, you're not dealing with poor performance; you're dealing with tension that seems to come out of thin air.

Funny enough, neither person is wrong. This is why personality clashes are so dangerous as they feel personal, but they're really not, they're about style, not substance. The way someone communicates, reacts under stress, or even how they run a meeting can trigger others without even realizing it.

Now, some of the most powerful teams are made of wildly different personalities. The key is knowing how to harness those differences instead of letting them explode into drama. So, when you spot a personality clash, don't diagnose it as conflict just yet, ask yourself:

- "Is this about values or just about style?"
- "Have we ever named the difference, or are they just silently frustrated with each other?"
- "Do they understand how they're wired and how others are too?"

Sometimes a single conversation, a little self-awareness, and a bit of coaching can turn friction into synergy. However, if left unchecked? These clashes can snowball into deeper resentment, which does then evolve into full-blown relationship-based conflict and that's when things get really tough. So, address it early before it gets infected.

METHODS OF CONFLICT RESOLUTION

How you respond to conflict tells your team more about your leadership than any strategy deck or vision statement ever will. You can talk culture all day, but if you blow up over small issues, go silent when your team needs a voice, or keep sacrificing the truth to keep the peace, they'll see right through you.

Now, there isn't one perfect method for handling conflict; great leaders adapt. They don't just react; they choose their weapons carefully, based on the war in front of them. Over the years, five main strategies have stood the test of time. Let's walk through them a bit:

First up is the infamous "avoid it and hope it dies" method. This one gets a bad rap, but it's not always a sign of weakness. There are moments where silence is wisdom. If the issue is small or the room is emotionally flooded, pulling back can be strategic. Some conflicts just need space, not speeches. I've seen smart leaders avoid unnecessary explosions by saying, "Let's give this 24 hours," and that one move saved morale, trust, and sanity. However, let me be clear, avoidance is a scalpel, not a shield. If you use it to dodge every hard conversation, you become the leader who disappears when it matters most. That kind of behavior doesn't just kill trust, it breeds cultural cancer. Teams stop speaking up, toxic people flourish, and small issues become landmines. Use avoidance like salt; sparingly, strategically, and never as the main course.

Now contrast that with accommodation. This one sounds noble: you let the other person have their way, you deescalate things, and you look like the peacemaker. There are definitely times this works when the relationship matters more than the issue, or when it's not worth lighting a fire over something that doesn't change the outcome. However, when accommodation becomes your default setting, you're just a doormat with a title. The kind of leader who keeps saying "okay" even when everything inside screams "no" will eventually explode or implode, and neither is fun to watch. I've seen leaders accommodate for years, then one day blow up over something tiny, not because it mattered, but because they finally snapped after a thousand tiny compromises. That's not leadership, that's emotional debt.

Then there's the classic competitor, the bulldog who has to win every argument, every decision, every meeting. There's a time for this. In a crisis, when speed matters more than consensus, or when you're defending core values, stepping in with firm direction can be heroic, but if you compete on everything, you create a battlefield where every team member feels like a soldier, not a contributor. They start holding back, playing it safe, or worse, waiting for you to decide everything so they don't get bulldozed. You don't want to be that leader. Winning the moment and losing the team is a terrible trade.

Let's talk compromise. Now, this one gets overused by nice leaders who think being fair is the same as being effective. "Let's meet halfway." It sounds good, doesn't it? However, halfway can still be the wrong place. If neither side is truly satisfied, or if the solution is watered down into mediocrity, then what you've done is delay conflict, not resolve it. I once saw a team compromise on a client strategy that made no one happy, and guess what, the campaign bombed. They had no conviction because no one truly believed in the plan. So yes, compromise has its place, especially when time is short, but don't use it as a default. It should be a tool, not a crutch.

And finally, the real MVP of conflict resolution: collaboration. This one's not fast, but it's powerful. When done right, collaboration takes longer but produces gold. You sit down, get the real issues on the table, and work toward a solution that doesn't just work, it honors what matters to everyone involved. This is the approach that builds trust, strengthens culture, and produces decisions people rally around (Cote, 2023). I've seen tension between product and engineering teams melt away when leadership said, "We're not picking sides. We're fixing the system together." That's collaboration, although let's not romanticize it; this only works when both parties are willing to show up with honesty, curiosity, and a shared desire to win together.

If one person is manipulative or defensive, collaboration turns into a fake dance where nothing changes.

Here's the real leadership play: know your style, but don't get married to it. Adapt, read the room, learn when to step back, when to stand firm, when to listen, and when to lead., because conflict, if you let it, can actually be the doorway to stronger relationships, clearer expectations, and deeper trust only if you walk through it not around it.

The Positivity of Conflict

That truth doesn't just echo in books or leadership workshops, it plays out in real, high-stakes environments where teams either grow up through tension or break apart because no one knows how to handle it. For instance:

Abraham Lincoln is one of the most profound examples of leadership shaped through conflict. He led the United States through its bloodiest war, held together a nation on the brink of collapse, and carried the burden of impossible choices — often alone. But what made Lincoln's leadership extraordinary wasn't just his decisions under fire. It was how he dealt with disagreement.

He intentionally surrounded himself with people who opposed him — a "Team of Rivals." Men who had run against him, doubted him, and publicly criticized him were brought into his cabinet. He didn't silence them. He listened. He debated. He made room for conflict not as a threat, but as a tool.

That tension sharpened his thinking, clarified his convictions, and kept him grounded in purpose. He understood that avoiding conflict for the sake of peace was just a slower path to collapse.

The lesson? Conflict doesn't have to be the breaking point. It can be the breakthrough. With enough courage and emotional maturity, leaders don't just survive tension — they emerge refined by it. Lincoln didn't run from disagreement. He led through it. And because of that, he didn't just preserve a country — he reshaped its future.

Another one, Joan of Arc—a symbol of bravery in the face of relentless conflict. At just 17, she led the French army to critical victories during the Hundred Years' War, but her greatest conflict wasn't just military, it was also a religious and political conflict. Despite being a peasant, she was able to influence the highest leaders, including Charles VII, by claiming divine guidance.

When she was captured by the English, Joan was put on trial and ultimately executed. Her unwavering commitment to her cause despite the political and personal threats she faced speaks volumes about resilience and self-belief. But even more powerful was her ability to hold firm to her values during her trial, where she engaged with her accusers, defended her faith, and didn't compromise on her mission despite the intense pressure.

Joan's conflict resolution lies in her steadfast leadership amidst overwhelming adversity. She didn't engage in negotiation with her enemies because of her unwavering mission, but she did use her platform for deep conviction to inspire her troops and future leaders to rise to their purpose, even in the face of death.

One final example: Wangari Maathai, the Nobel Peace Prize-winning environmental and political activist, who faced significant conflict in her fight to protect Kenya's environment, most notably the Green Belt Movement. The movement aimed to combat deforestation while empowering women, but it was met with fierce opposition from the government, which saw the movement as a threat to its power.

Despite the government's aggressive attempts to stop her, including harassment, imprisonment, and discrediting campaigns, Maathai stood firm. She knew that the conflicts she was enduring were necessary to bring about long-term social, political, and environmental change. She didn't avoid confrontation; instead, she embraced it as part of the journey. What's key in her story is the way she handled conflict with grace, often addressing unresolved issues with the government, but without getting lost in bitterness or anger.

Her resolution strategies were staying focused on the long-term goals, remaining principled despite personal challenges, and always looking for win-win outcomes. She never wavered, even in the face of harsh resistance, showing how conflict, when managed with vision and steadfast dedication, can lead to greater good.

In all of these stories, we see leaders who didn't shy away from conflict, but instead used it as a tool for growth, transformation, and success. Whether it's Lincoln navigating civil war, Joan of Arc defying political and spiritual opposition, or Wangari Maathai standing against corrupt systems — great leaders don't run from conflict. They use it.

Not to destroy — but to transform.

Embracing Conflict

There was a season where everything in the business was growing, except the team. We had the revenue and momentum but underneath the surface, people were quietly frustrated, forming cliques, avoiding each other in meetings, and hiding behind vague emails. I could feel the tension every Monday morning for quite a long time. Smiles felt forced, feedback was filtered, and collaboration became political.

The turning point came in the middle of a product launch.

Our head of engineering clashed hard with our lead designer. On the surface, it was about deadlines but underneath, it was cultural. One was an ex-corporate perfectionist who valued systems and structure and the other was a free-spirited creative who hated being boxed in. The arguments were heated then one day, I found out they had gone two weeks without speaking directly, only communicating through Slack and passive-aggressive comments in shared docs.

At first, I tried to mediate quietly through one-on-ones and small nudges, but it didn't work. Eventually, I called a full team meeting to air the tension. I opened the floor and said, "This is not about features. This is about fear. Fear of being misunderstood, fear of not being heard, fear of not being respected." Then I stepped back and let people talk.

Believe me, it was raw; people cried to a point, one even walked out. But then, something shifted. In the days that followed, I started seeing small signs of healing, Slack messages that were more human, side conversations that were less guarded. We eventually hired a facilitator and did a full team workshop off-site. We cooked together, shared stories about our backgrounds, and talked about the cultures we came from, the trauma we carried, and the things we feared most in a team setting. We even created a conflict playbook together—not just what we'd tolerate, but how we'd deal with friction.

I'll never forget one teammate who said, "This is the first time I've felt safe bringing my whole self to work."

Conflict didn't disappear after that, but it matured. Instead of ghosting each other or spiraling into blame, people started leaning in. We normalized healthy disagreement, and just like that, I started seeing team members proactively book time to "clear the air." Feedback became more honest and more generous.

That chapter taught me that conflict isn't something you fix, it's something you facilitate and it starts at the top. You don't need to have all the answers, you just need to create an environment where the hard stuff can surface without shame. A place where people don't have to pretend everything is fine to be seen as valuable.

Sometimes, leadership is less about solving conflict and more about holding space for people to grow through it.

Here's how you start building that kind of space, starting Monday.

MONDAY MORNING
PLAYBOOK

Great teams don't avoid conflict, they leverage it. If you're flinching at every bit of tension, you're not leading, you're surviving. Conflict is where culture is tested and trust is built. Master it, and you master the team.

🧠 MINDSET SHIFT:

Conflict isn't the enemy; unresolved conflict is. High-performing teams don't sidestep disagreements; they confront them head-on, fix them, and get stronger.

✓ DO THIS MONDAY:

1. Identify the Tension Points (By End of Day Today)

- Walk the floor. Listen. Where are the bottlenecks? Who's not communicating?
- Write down the three biggest sources of tension on your team right now. If you can't name them, you're disconnected.
- Bring these up in your next team huddle and say it straight: "Here's what I'm seeing. Let's address it."

2. Schedule a Conflict Workshop (This Week)

- Call it what it is: Conflict Mastery Session.
- Gather the key players involved in the tension. You're not there to referee, you're there to surface truth and build solutions.
- Use this format:
  - What's the real issue here?
  - What assumptions are we making?
  - What needs to change for this to get resolved?

3. Establish a Conflict Playbook (This Month)

- Write it down. Create a one-pager for your team on how conflict will be handled moving forward:
  - Immediate Address: Conflicts are brought up within 48 hours, no festering.
  - Direct Communication: No middlemen, no Slack sniping.
  - Resolution Window: If it's not resolved in two weeks, it escalates.
  - Public Acknowledgment: Wins and resolutions get publicly praised.

CHAPTER 7:

MANAGING THE TOUGH STUFF – UNDERPERFORMANCE AND TOXICITY

"The standard you walk past is the standard you accept."
– Lt. Gen. David Morrison

In 1997, the Chicago Bulls were at the top of the world—five championships in seven years, the best player alive, and a coach who defined modern basketball leadership. Yet, there was Dennis Rodman behind the rings: wildly talented, absolutely unpredictable, and constantly pushing the line.

Here's the twist: Phil Jackson never ignored Rodman's behavior. He managed it with hard conversations, boundaries, and accountability. He knew that if you let chaos slide, it slides straight into your culture even when you're winning.

That's the difference between leaders who preserve culture and those who poison it by pretending problems will just go away. They won't. Whether it's a disrespectful employee, under-the-radar toxicity, unchecked ego, or someone just quietly slipping below the standard, you're either dealing with it or you're letting it become how things are done around here.

Let me say this plainly:

Every problem you ignore becomes a policy. Every behavior you excuse becomes a belief system.

Leaders love talking about "culture" in interviews, brand decks, and office murals, but culture isn't built in a workshop; it's built in the conflict. It's built in that awkward moment when someone makes a passive-aggressive jab in a meeting, and you either stop it or let it linger. It's built when a high performer starts acting like they're untouchable, and you either coach their humility or feed their ego.

The scary part is that cultural erosion is slow and subtle. It doesn't always come with alarms, but trust me, if you're not paying attention, the whole foundation will rot before you realize what happened.

So, let this be the reckoning; we're not here to sugarcoat, hide, or cope, we're here to confront because the tough stuff isn't the side mission, it's the main quest. Whether it's a rogue superstar poisoning morale, a solid employee slipping into a slump, or a brewing feud between two teammates, you've got two options: Deal with it or let it define your team.

UNDERPERFORMANCE

Let's paint a picture.

Imagine you've got someone on your team—let's call her Rachel. When she started, she was on fire. Hustled hard and brought ideas. She stayed late without being asked, but over the past few months... something's changed. Tasks slip, energy's flat, she misses small details she used to nail. The team notices, and so do you, but every time you think about addressing it, something else comes up. You justify it to yourself—"She's been loyal, maybe it's burnout, so I'll give it more time."

And just like that, what started as a minor slip turns into a performance crater.

This is the cost of delay. Underperformance that goes unaddressed doesn't stay neutral; it spreads. It demoralizes high performers, disrupts workflow, and slowly chips away at your standards. The team starts asking: Why should I give my best when others can coast?

Underperformance isn't just an individual issue, it's a leadership test. How you respond sets the tone for the whole team.

Understanding the Roots of Underperformance

Before you rush into correction mode, pause and diagnose. Not all underperformance is laziness or bad intent. In fact, even your best people will underperform at some point in their journey. Life happens, environments shift, or expectations change. So, here are some of the common root causes:

- Lack of clarity – They don't know what success looks like anymore.
- Burnout or disengagement – They've lost the fire and are silently suffering.
- Mismatched role – They're in the wrong seat on the bus.

- Skill gaps – They were promoted or hired above their readiness.
- Personal issues – Mental health, relationships, or finances bleeding into work.
- Weak onboarding or feedback – They were never truly set up for success.

You're not babysitting, but you are still responsible for identifying whether the issue is will or skill, or something deeper. Here's where great leaders earn their stripes. You don't jump straight to warnings and ultimatums, you build a coaching rhythm that escalates with both compassion and consequence. Below is a simple ladder you can use to help someone climb up through the process:

Step	Action	Goal	Tone
Clarify Expectations	Revisit the role, KPIs, and what "great" looks like.	Eliminate ambiguity. Reset the standard.	Neutral, clear.
Coach With Support	Offer tools, time, and guidance. Have regular check-ins.	Reinforce belief and offer help.	Encouraging but firm.
Raise Accountability	Introduce timelines, tighter metrics, and consequences for no change.	Add urgency without shame.	Serious, direct.
Final Chance Conversation	One last honest conversation. No sugarcoating.	Draw the line. Make the choice clear.	Stern but respectful.
Release or Redeploy	Either part ways or shift to a role they can thrive in.	Protect team and culture.	Professional, decisive.

This ladder is simply a toolkit to help you give each person a chance to rise, and should they choose not to, you made space, and you led with integrity.

However, some leaders avoid this process altogether. They hope things will fix themselves whereas time rarely heals underperformance, it compounds it instead. When you delay action, you send mixed signals to your team and reward mediocrity with silence. Waiting may feel like kindness but often, it's just fear dressed up as patience.

You're not doing anyone a favor by keeping someone in a role they're failing at. They know it, you know it, and your silence slowly becomes a betrayal of them and of your team. Essentially, good leaders coach. Great leaders confront with clarity, compassion, and 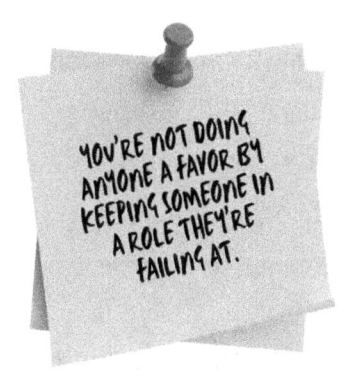 consequences. So don't flinch, your credibility is forged in these moments. Underperformance doesn't fix itself; the right kind of leadership can either redeem it or release it. Either way, you win.

There was this top performer on our sales team, crushed targets for two quarters straight. Everyone respected her grind, I mean, she literally had that it factor. Then, slowly, she started checking out. First it was skipping meetings, then missing internal deadlines. Energy dipped while I just thought, "She's earned some slack, she'll find her rhythm again."

However, the problem wasn't burnout, it was entitlement. She believed her past wins gave her permission to coast, and worse, to dismiss accountability. The rest of the team noticed it which led to resentment growing. One teammate even told me, "If she can get away with it, why should I keep pushing?"

By the time I stepped in, the culture had already taken a hit. I had to reverse a pattern I'd unintentionally allowed. The conversation was tough but necessary. What I learned was that past performance can't excuse present disengagement. No one is above the standard, not even your star players.

But what happens when the problem isn't performance but presence? When someone's work might be solid, but their energy is off? That's when you're not just managing output, you're managing ego. And trust me, ego can do just as much damage as incompetence. Maybe more.

CUTTING THE CANCER – REMOVE TOXICITY BEFORE IT SPREADS

Have you ever seen what mold does in a house? At first, it's hidden, maybe in the wall, under the sink, or just behind the drywall. Quiet and barely noticeable, but if left alone, it spreads, rots the structure, breeds illness, and eventually, that house you spent years building becomes unlivable. That's what a toxic employee does. Funnily enough, usually they're not loud about it, they smile in meetings, cc you on emails, and they might even hit their numbers just enough to stay under the radar. Yet, behind the scenes, they're gossiping, undermining, whispering doubt, poisoning belief, and killing energy. These people are cancers, and if you don't remove them, your entire team suffers. Furthermore, what they do is:

- Drain your top performers who are trying to stay positive.
- Influence the "silent middle" who just want peace, pushing them toward apathy.
- Question leadership subtly enough to make others feel unsure, even when you're doing the right thing.

Let's be crystal clear: You do not get extra points for tolerating toxicity in the name of "loyalty" or "second chances." That's not leadership, that's cowardice dressed in compassion, and trust me, your good employees see it. They won't say anything, but they're watching. Every day you let that cancer sit in the corner, infecting morale, you lose a little more of your team's belief in you. So, in everything you do, always be cognizant that culture isn't built by what you preach, it's built by what you tolerate (Willink, n.d.-a). Let that sink in for a moment.

Now, deep down you know you should fire them, so why haven't you? Maybe they've been around since the early days or maybe they're good at their job but toxic in attitude. Maybe you're afraid of the confrontation or of what happens when they leave but then experience has taught me that keeping the wrong person is always more expensive than replacing them. Always. Remember, they don't just hurt your results, they hurt your people.

KEEPING THE WRONG PERSON IS ALWAYS MORE EXPENSIVE THAN REPLACING THEM. ALWAYS.

For instance, in 2018, NBA All-Star Jimmy Butler was a rising star, but in Minnesota, he became infamous for tearing into his teammates during practice, berating younger players, calling out the coach, and creating a tense locker room (Collier, 2025). Even though he was producing on the court, the culture was eroding. He was eventually traded, and what happened next? The team improved their chemistry almost immediately, and Butler landed in Miami and thrived in a culture built for his intensity.

The lesson here is that culture fit matters. It's not about talent alone, it's also about what they bring into the locker room, the office, the team, or the workspace.

So, how do we handle such toxicity?

1. **Watch closely.** These people rarely mess up publicly. Get feedback from multiple team members and also look for behavioral patterns, not just performance metrics.

2. **Call it out directly.** Don't dance around it. Use Radical Candor—care personally, challenge directly.

3. **Give one opportunity for correction.** Not five, one.

4. **If they double down, let them go.** And do it clean without drama, gossip, just clarity.

Again, your job is not to babysit grown adults with bad attitudes but to protect the mission. Every day you keep a toxic person, you're quietly frustrating and firing the good ones, so choose wisely because your team already knows who the cancer is. The only question is, what are *you* going to do about it?

The Balance Between Patience and Decisiveness

Every leader will eventually find themselves walking a tightrope between patience and decisiveness. Get this balance wrong, and it can cost you your culture, your credibility, or even your company.

Move too quickly, and you risk making rash, emotionally driven decisions that alienate loyal people or cut short someone's potential. Wait too long, and the damage multiplies; one small issue quietly becomes a large, team-wide infection.

Great leaders develop the wisdom to know when to pause and when to act. They do not fall into the extremes of impulsiveness or passivity. Instead, they learn to recognize the moment for what it is and respond with courage, clarity, and strategy.

Two Dangerous Extremes: Impulsiveness vs Paralysis

Leadership decisions are rarely clean-cut. There is always nuance, emotion, and uncertainty, but two extremes tend to show up when pressure is high. Impulsiveness is the tendency to act quickly, without reflection or investigation. It often comes from frustration or fear. Leaders who operate impulsively may terminate an employee after one incident, snap at someone without hearing the full story, or make sweeping changes based on emotion rather than facts. This type of leadership creates instability. People walk on eggshells, and good team members become afraid to take risks or speak up (Pacelli, 2021).

On the other end is paralysis, where the leader delays necessary decisions under the guise of caution. They overthink, over-process, and convince themselves that waiting is wisdom but what actually happens is decay (Laoyan, 2025). Problems grow, morale dips, and credibility erodes. The team begins to wonder, "Does our leader actually see what's going on? Do they even care?"

Both of these extremes, impulsive reaction and fearful delay, are forms of emotional leadership. Neither builds strong teams nor builds trust. The real challenge is knowing when a situation calls for immediate action versus when it needs space to unfold. That tension is where true leadership lives.

Decisiveness is not the same as recklessness, and patience is not the same as avoidance. A decisive leader gathers enough data, considers context, consults with trusted voices when needed, and then moves firmly in the right direction. A patient leader gives space for growth, but still holds people accountable, still has hard conversations, and still moves things forward. True leadership decisions are often uncomfortable, and they certainly require conviction. You must be able to look beyond the moment and ask, "What is best for the culture?", "What is best for the mission?", and "What message will this decision send to the rest of the team?"

When Patience Is Wise

There are several scenarios where patience is not only appropriate but essential.

- **A strong performer hits a rough patch.** Perhaps they are going through personal challenges or burnout. Their track record has earned them grace.
- **A new hire is struggling to adjust.** They may need more coaching, feedback, or clarity before they can thrive.

- **A conflict arises, but both parties are open to resolution.** With the right facilitation, this can be a chance to strengthen relationships.
- **An error is made due to inexperience, not negligence.** Mistakes are part of growth, and how you respond will shape your team's learning culture.

In these situations, leading with empathy, clarity, and accountability helps build trust and long-term loyalty. It's a moment to coach, not to cut.

When Decisiveness Is Required

However, there are situations where swift action is not just recommended, it is nonnegotiable.

- **There is a breach of trust.** Lying, stealing, manipulation, or repeated dishonesty cannot be tolerated.
- **Toxic behaviors are affecting others.** Gossip, sabotage, bullying, or ego-driven disruptions must be addressed immediately.
- **There is ongoing underperformance with no effort to improve.** If someone consistently fails to meet expectations and resists feedback, your team pays the price.
- **You see a clear threat to culture or integrity.** These are not moments for reflection. They are moments for leadership.

Hesitation in these moments sends the wrong signal. It tells the rest of the team that harmful behavior will be tolerated and that the standards you preach are not the standards you enforce. That dissonance breaks trust faster than anything else.

The "Marinate Method"

Then, there are also times when you do not yet have enough data to act decisively. This is where the principle of "marinating" becomes useful. This method does not mean avoiding or ignoring the issue; it means intentionally giving it space to reveal itself more fully. You observe, have an initial conversation, set a clear expectation, track progress, and then let patterns surface. When you finally make your move, it is firm, informed, and final. Letting something marinate allows you to make decisions with clarity rather than emotion (Anderson, 2014). It doesn't necessarily mean stalling, it's simply about leading with precision.

This is the leadership dance. It's not easy, but the stakes are high. Handle the moment well, and your team learns to trust your judgment. Handle it poorly, and that trust begins to crumble.

When Ego Takes the Wheel, Culture Crashes

Ego is not a quirk, it's a culture killer.

Some leaders treat ego like it's a personality trait to manage around; "Oh, that's just how Sarah is." No. Ego is one of the most dangerous liabilities on a team, and I've seen it firsthand. The meetings that suddenly get quieter when a certain someone walks in, the eye rolls teammates exchange when that person speaks, and the ideas that never get voiced because someone else insists on being the loudest. You may think they're just confident or excuse it because they get results, but let me be clear: ego doesn't build teams—it burns them from the inside out.

This isn't just business, it's human nature. Look at Anakin Skywalker; the Chosen One, gifted, powerful, and unstoppable, but the moment his ego eclipsed his purpose, he didn't just fall, he turned from Jedi to Darth Vader, from savior to destroyer. All this because ego doesn't want to serve, it wants to be worshipped, and when you lead a team, you don't need gods, you need teammates.

Same story plays out in sports. Look at Russell Westbrook during his prime OKC years—elite talent, MVP-level impact, but there were moments when his sheer will to dominate overshadowed his ability to integrate. The assist numbers were there, sure, but so were the forced plays, the iso-ball, the "me-against-the-world" energy. Talent can elevate a team, but ego? Ego isolates it, my friend.

So, what do you do? How do you coach the ego without crushing the soul?

Well, start by holding up the mirror. You don't attack the person, you invite reflection. Ask questions like, "How do you think others experience you in meetings?" and "What role do you see yourself playing on this team?" You need to make them *feel* their impact, not just hear about it, because transformation starts with self-awareness.

Then, call out patterns, not personalities. Don't label them "difficult" or "egotistical." That's lazy leadership; instead, say, "I've noticed you tend to dismiss your teammates' ideas in strategy sessions; what's behind that?" You name the behavior, then open a door to growth. Furthermore, always, always tie it back to the mission. Remind them: "No one wins solo, we're all here to win together. Your brilliance isn't being questioned, but your buy-in is." Ego needs to understand that it's not the engine, it's just one part of the machine.

Now, this next part is critical; you set the bar, and you set it hard. "On this team, collaboration and humility aren't optional. You don't have to like everyone, but you do have to respect them. Period." And you don't give it six months to play out, you give it a short runway; one-on-ones, real conversations, and clear expectations.

However, if the ego still resists and the same patterns keep showing up, then it's time to draw the line because no amount of performance is worth a poisoned culture. I don't care if they're your top closer, your most seasoned exec, or the one who "built the system." If their presence consistently damages trust, stifles collaboration, or demoralizes others, then they go. You may think you can't afford to lose them, I promise you: you can't afford to keep them.

Your real stars are watching and if you let ego thrive, you'll slowly lose the ones who actually make the culture work so you confront it, you coach it, and if it won't change-you cut it.

End of story.

Now this is when you start cutting unapologetically.

Coach or Cut? How Real Leaders Decide

The Gut-Level Discernment Every Leader Must Develop

Let's not sugarcoat it: Some people are just not worth the rescue mission, and if you're a fixer by nature, this is where you'll get hurt because you'll see *potential* in everyone. You'll believe that with enough time, care, and feedback, they'll turn the corner. Unfortunately, some people don't want to be coached, they want to be coddled and the longer you entertain that, the more your team bleeds.

You need a system, but more than that, you need instincts. This is art and science; discernment over documentation. So, how do you know who's coachable… and who's a cultural liability dressed in potential?

Coach the hungry, cut the entitled.
If someone still shows up with curiosity, asks questions, and owns their missteps even if they're messy, they're worth the time because that's a confirmation of the presence of a rare raw material called humility. However, if they think feedback is beneath them, if they treat accountability like an insult, if they drain your team's energy every time they open their mouth, that's not a project—that's a problem.

Watch what happens after the first confrontation.
You want to know who's coachable? Don't look at how they react in the moment. Look at what they do after. Do they reflect? Adjust? Seek clarity? Or do they sulk, deflect, and gossip in the corners of the office? The aftermath tells you everything.

Look for patterns, not potential.
Potential is seductive, but patterns don't lie. Has this person consistently underdelivered? Do they blame others more than they own outcomes? Do you trust them to carry the culture in your absence, or do you feel like you're babysitting a grown-up with a title?

Listen to your team's silence.

Sometimes your people won't tell you what they really feel, but they'll show you. They'll go quiet, then engagement dips, and creativity dies. If the room always tenses up around one person, trust that tension, energy is data. And let's be real, this isn't just about the bad hires; sometimes, the toughest calls involve people you like. People who've been with you since the early days, people who helped build the thing. Remember, you're not just leading individuals, you're protecting a system.

So, when in doubt, ask yourself this: *"If I met this person today, knowing everything I know now, would I still hire them?"*

If the answer is no, then why are they still here?

Fail fast, but don't fail blind. You owe it to your team and to your own sanity to make the hard call. Sometimes, the most loving thing you can do for them and for your culture is to show them the door. After all, leadership isn't just about building great teams, it's about protecting them from the ones who don't want to grow.

WHEN LOYALTY CLOUDS LEADERSHIP

One of my hardest leadership lessons came from hiring a long-time friend—let's call him Dale. We'd known each other for nearly two decades. When I needed a Director of Operations, I thought he was the perfect fit. I trusted him and believed in his experience. I assumed that because we'd walked through life together, we'd be unstoppable at work.

I was wrong.

From the beginning, Dale struggled. He bulldozed conversations, dismissed others' ideas, and made comments that crossed lines. Worse, when things went south, he reached for the friendship card instead of taking responsibility.

And I let him.

I made excuses and defended him to the rest of the team. Told myself I could coach him through it. What I didn't realize then was that my loyalty wasn't just protecting Dale, it was quietly corroding everything else. The team saw it and the standard shifted. The culture bent and when people stopped believing I'd treat everyone fairly, they started pulling back from me too.

Eventually, I had to let Dale go, but by then, the damage was done; his role, his credibility, and even our friendship didn't survive. That part still hurts to this day.

But here's the truth that now anchors me: Leadership isn't just about being fair, it's about being seen as fair, and when you protect one person at the expense of the standard, you lose far more than you save.

If you want to build a loyal team, start by refusing to show favoritism. If someone's failing the culture, it doesn't matter if they're a star, a genius, or your best friend from third grade. Hold the line because if you don't, your team will walk away long before they tell you.

So, you've got some serious thinking to do this week. Don't rush past this. Don't skim it. And don't skip it. Grab your notebook, clear some space, and get surgical. Before you dive into the Monday Morning Playbook, I want you to sit with this and begin a long-term exercise that will shape how you lead. Here's how I suggest you get started:

1. **Audit your team.**

   List your top five most difficult personalities. Now ask: Are they coachable, or are they quietly contaminating the room? Be brutally honest.

2. **Reflect on your own loyalty traps.**

   Is there anyone you're protecting because of history, not performance? Ask yourself: If they were a new hire, would they still have a job?

3. **Set one courageous conversation.**

   Who do you need to confront this week? Ego, entitlement, or disengagement—pick one. Prepare, don't procrastinate.

4. **Redefine the standard publicly.**

   At your next team meeting, reset the cultural tone. Remind your team that standards apply to *everyone*. No exemptions, no favorites.

5. **Decide: coach or cut.**

   If you've already tried coaching someone and nothing's changed, why are they still here? Don't delay. Culture isn't neutral; it's either reinforced or eroded every day.

MONDAY MORNING
PLAYBOOK

If you don't deal with it, it becomes your culture.

MINDSET SHIFT:

Avoiding a tough conversation doesn't protect your culture, it poisons it. Your silence is permission, and your inaction is endorsement. The longer you wait, the worse it gets.

✓ DO THIS MONDAY:

1. Identify the "Culture Killer" You've Been Tolerating (By End of Day Today)

- You already know who or what it is. That person who's always undermining the team, that behavior you let slide because it's "just the way they are."
- Ask yourself: If someone great joined the team today, would this person drive them away?
- If the answer is yes, address it right away. Schedule a one-on-one and get real about the damage it's causing.

2. Coach Before You Cut (This Week)

- If someone's underperforming, you don't ghost them into failure, you coach them into clarity.
- Schedule a direct one-on-one and lay it out:
  - "Here's what's expected."
  - "Here's where we're missing."
  - "Let's talk about how we're going to fix it."
- Be ruthless about expectations, but clear about support. If you haven't given them a path to improvement, you haven't led; you've just judged.

3. Set Boundaries Around Ego (Today)

- Call out behavior that's self-serving, dismissive, or team-destructive.
- Say this directly: "This can't be about winning arguments, it has to be about winning as a team."
- If ego is running the room, you're not. Shut it down before it spreads. Culture is more fragile than you think.

CHAPTER 8:

SCALING & SUSTAINING SUCCESS – BUILDING A TEAM THAT GROWS WITH YOUR BUSINESS

"The best executive is the one who has sense enough to pick good men to do what he wants done, and self-restraint enough to keep from meddling with them while they do it."
— Theodore Roosevelt

There comes a moment in every leader's journey when the very things that made them successful start to become the things that hold them back. You feel it before you can explain it: meetings get messier, decisions get delayed, balls start dropping, and the hustle that once felt exhilarating now feels exhausting. You look around and realize that you're not building a business anymore—you're babysitting one.

Let's call it what it is: You built your company through sweat, instinct, late nights, and sheer willpower. You wore every hat, closed every deal, and fixed every screw-up. You were the firestarter, the glue, the engine, and the shock absorber, and that worked perfectly-until it didn't.

Hustle is what gets you off the ground, but it's structure that gets you through the ceiling. If you're still trying to scale your business by being involved in everything, you're not leading; you're hoarding, and eventually, the business will choke on your need to be central. You'll become the bottleneck. The culture will fray, and your best people will leave not because you're a bad leader, but because you refused to evolve.

Leadership at scale isn't about doing more, it's about designing better. It's about replacing control with clarity. Hustle with systems. Presence with process. You have to move from the front lines to the blueprint and from being the MVP to being the architect of a team that can win without you in the room. I've seen founders make this shift and explode their growth. I've also seen leaders cling to control and become the very reason their business stalled. You've got to make a decision: Are you going to be the fuel… or the foundation? Because you can't be both forever.

Real leadership is knowing when to step back so others can step up. It's designing the engine instead of being the piston. It's building a system that doesn't just carry your vision but multiplies it. This is where everything changes. The tools, the mindset, the people, the rhythm. This is the stretch where you stop thinking like a founder and start operating like a CEO, and the faster you embrace that shift, the stronger and more scalable your business becomes.

THE TRANSITION FROM SMALL TO LARGE TEAMS

When your team is small, your leadership is personal. You see, hear, and fix everything. At this point, you're not managing culture, you *are* the culture. Every issue flows through you, and every success has your fingerprints on it. However, once the business grows past a certain size, that intimacy becomes unsustainable. You don't just need more people, you need a different kind of leadership.

You're no longer the star player, you're becoming the head coach. That means the job changes; you stop calling plays on the field and start building the playbook. You're not in every huddle, but you're designing the system that guides every huddle. The shift is massive and if you don't make it, your company starts to choke on its own growth.

Think of it like this: When you're a chef running a food truck, you can touch every plate, taste every sauce, fix every mistake, but when you open a full-blown restaurant with a team of 20, that hands-on approach becomes the problem. You're not supposed to be on the line anymore, you're supposed to be designing the operations, training sous-chefs, and creating standards that deliver quality at scale. If you keep trying to do it all, orders back up, the kitchen melts down, and customers walk.

The same thing happens in business, if you don't evolve from operator to orchestrator, you become the bottleneck. You're not scaling, you're suffocating.

A good example is Stripe—one of the most successful fintech start-ups in the world, and one reason for this is their obsessive focus on scaling structure in step with growth. In the early years, founders Patrick and John Collison could sit in on most hiring interviews and approve every product update. As Stripe exploded, they shifted their posture entirely, building tight layers of leadership. They empowered teams to own outcomes, and critically, they installed strong "operating principles" that clarified how decisions should be made without the founders in the room. That's why Stripe didn't just grow fast, it grew with consistency, even as complexity multiplied.

That's your goal, too: to scale without diluting what made your business great in the first place. That said, this requires the humility to stop being the hero and start being the architect.

Scaling isn't just about hiring more people, it's about becoming a different kind of leader.

Most leaders stall because they cling to the leadership style that got them to 5 or 15 people, but then what gets you to 50 or 500 is an entirely different game. Here's a breakdown of how your leadership must evolve across each stage of team growth. Use this as a mirror, not a map, to challenge your current habits and shift gears as your company scales.

Leadership Evolution Table

Stage	Team Size	Role Focus	Decision-Making Style	Biggest Risk	Key Leadership
Hustler	1–5	Doing everything yourself	Centralized (all through you)	Burnout, bottlenecking	Ownership
Player-Coach	6–15	Leading while doing	Partial delegation	Blurred roles, inconsistent standards	Adaptability
Head Coach	16–50	Leading leaders	Delegated with accountability	Culture drift, middle-manager gap	Strategic clarity
Architect	50–500+	Designing systems & culture	Distributed, system-driven	Losing soul, over-complexity	Intentionality

Each of these transitions, whether from hustler to strategist, or from fixer to coach, isn't just about changing what you do but changing how you think. Scaling isn't just a systems game, it's a leadership transformation and as you step into this next level, you'll quickly realize something else: the true bottleneck isn't the market, or the model, it's you. Your capacity to let go, to empower, and to trust others will determine how far your business can really go.

Which brings us to one of the hardest but most liberating pillars of scale: delegation.

DELEGATION – LETTING GO TO GROW

There's a lie that far too many leaders carry like gospel: "If I want it done right, I have to do it myself." It sounds noble and feels responsible, but it's the seed of burnout and the beginning of bottleneck leadership.

In the early days, this mindset was almost necessary. When you're in the trenches, building something from scratch, every detail runs through you. You're the one answering customer emails, tweaking product features, reviewing marketing copy, and closing the books at midnight. You're not just running the business, you are the business.

However, as the business scales, that mentality becomes a liability. What once made you effective now makes you exhausted. The same hustle that built your company begins to strangle it. Growth exposes the unsustainable truth that you can't scale while still trying to touch everything.

This is where the shift must happen from operator to orchestrator. You don't stop caring, you stop controlling. You stop hoarding responsibilities and start distributing ownership. That's the heart of true delegation. Not task-dumping. Not "do this because I said so." Rather, it's all about entrusting others to own outcomes. This enables them to think, to lead, and yes, sometimes to fail—because yes, failure is part of it. One of the hardest but most essential parts of delegation is watching someone drop the ball and resisting the urge to swoop in, because if you always save the day, you rob your team of the growth that comes from getting back up.

I once coached a founder who had grown his SaaS company to $3 million in revenue. On paper, everything looked great, but behind the scenes, he was spiraling. Every piece of copy, every marketing asset, every new hire, even the color palette of a slide deck, had to pass through him. His logic was simple: "I'm protecting the brand."

In reality, he was strangling it, and as a result, his team felt paralyzed. No one wanted to take initiative. Why would they, when they knew he'd redo their work anyway? People started pulling back, disengaging, quietly clocking out mentally, and he was burning out, resenting the very business he built.

Once we installed a real delegation framework—clear roles, defined outcomes, and permission to make decisions without running it all through him, everything changed. Within six months, his stress levels dropped, his team re-engaged, and the business broke through the $5M ceiling. Not because he worked harder, but because he let go.

So, you can either be the hero or the bottleneck, but you can't be both. Scaling requires a new identity. You're no longer the firefighter, you're the architect. Your job isn't to fix problems anymore, it's to build the system that prevents them in the first place. That means stepping back so others can step up. That means giving people room to grow, even if they stumble.

Letting go might feel like losing something at first: quality, speed, certainty, but what you gain is far greater: time, trust, leadership, and scale, because a business that requires your touch on everything is a business that will never outgrow you.

So, take a moment and ask yourself: What are you currently holding onto that someone else on your team could own with the right coaching, the right clarity, and the space to rise?

If you don't start handing off the baton, your race ends with you. Each of these transitions, whether from hustler to strategist or from fixer to coach, isn't just about changing what you do but simply evolving who you are. Scaling a business is impossible if you're not also scaling yourself. The reason we've been sharpening your coaching instincts throughout this journey isn't just for your team's sake, it's for your own transformation. You can't lead others to grow if you've stopped growing yourself.

Staying at the same level, in the same mindset, with the same hustle habits that got you through the early grind isn't leadership; that's stagnation. Goals aren't just for companies, they're for leaders too. You owe it to your team and to yourself to keep rising because the bigger the business gets, the more your role shifts from being in the trenches to becoming the shepherd for your company culture. Not the micromanager, not the martyr—the steady, visionary, accountable shepherd.

CREATING LAYERS OF LEADERSHIP WITHOUT LOSING CULTURE

A little mic drop moment: You can't build an empire with a village mindset.

When scaling, the battlefield changes; at this point, you need lieutenants, not loyal followers. Furthermore, scale isn't just adding people, it's about multiplying leadership

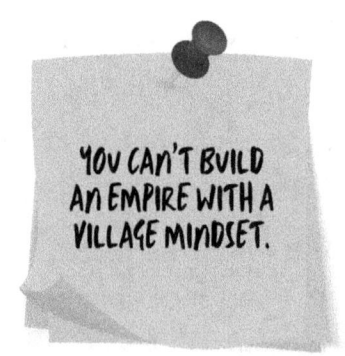

YOU CAN'T BUILD AN EMPIRE WITH A VILLAGE MINDSET.

and that requires designing intentional layers of influence, not just filling org charts with inflated titles.

Take another page from the Navy SEALs. They operate in fire teams of four to six because decision speed, accountability, and cohesion erode when a leader has too many people under them. Even in the chaos of war, they know: Clarity comes from compression and that means fewer direct reports, tighter pods, and higher trust.

Most companies ignore this, and they go on to promote the best individual contributor into a manager, give them 12 people to lead, and call it scaling. What they've really done is install a bottleneck with a fancy name.

The job of the founder now becomes to architect leadership bandwidth and build teams within the team. Your top performers shouldn't be reporting to you forever, they should become you. Not a copy of your personality, but a carrier of your principles, and that's where most leaders fall short. They grow obsessed with control instead of being obsessed with culture.

Now, you don't scale by controlling people, you scale by infecting them with a culture so strong they lead like you would even when you're not in the room. That's what the Golden State Warriors got right. When Steve Kerr took over, he didn't just run plays, he empowered voices. Draymond became the emotional engine, Steph set the tone for unselfish excellence, and Andre was the veteran compass. Layers, not just one voice at the top, but a culture that echoed through the locker room louder than the coach's clipboard.

So, if you want to scale, build that. Create leaders who own the culture, not just repeat it. If culture lives only in the founder, it dies in the hallway.

Here's how you build layers without losing your soul:

- Hire for cultural fidelity, not just competence. You don't need stars, you need standard-bearers.
- Set nonnegotiables, then give latitude. Core values are the bedrock, so let each leader adapt the rest.
- Make leadership a reward for multiplying, not just performing. Don't promote the hero, promote the one who creates heroes.
- Run leadership cadences, weekly syncs, one-on-ones, and scorecards.

You're no longer the fire, you're the spark. Your job is to light torches, not hold them all yourself.

So, ask yourself: Who are you shaping right now to carry the weight of your culture? Because trust me, the most dangerous place for a company to grow is without cultural shepherds at every level.

Your new KPI isn't just revenue, it's replication. Build a leadership factory or get buried by the very scale you prayed for.

Now comes the next evolution: keeping the infrastructure running without constant intervention. You've got leaders-great, now you need leverage. Not through more hustle but through structure, rhythm, and repeatability. This is where systems either scale you or strangle you.

Building Systems That Scale

If delegation is the muscle and leadership is the brain, then systems are the skeleton. Without them, everything collapses under its own weight.

At five people, you can wing it. At 15, you can hold it together with Slack messages, late-night texts, and memory, but once you start crossing 25, 40, 70 team members, that DIY duct-tape approach becomes a noose. You don't rise to the level of your hustle, you fall to the level of your systems (Clear, n.d.).

Most founders don't build systems because they think systems will slow them down. Well, what's really slowing them down is answering the same questions 10 times a week, rewriting processes from scratch, and constantly fighting fires they should've fireproofed long ago.

Systems aren't bureaucracy, they're freedom at scale.

Think about McDonald's—love or hate them, they've scaled globally; not by having the best burger but by having a system so precise, a 17-year-old in Cleveland can deliver a consistent product indistinguishable from one in Tokyo.

If you want predictable outcomes, then you need predictable input. That's what systems do. And no, I'm not talking about cold, rigid machines here; I'm talking about building repeatable greatness. Systems that don't suffocate people, but unlock them. That provide structure without stealing souls. That make winning less of a fluke and more of a rhythm.

Let's break this down:

- **Documented processes**: If it's done more than twice, write it down. Train your team to fish, not to ask for fish every week.
- **Clear decision rights**: Who decides what? At what level? No more "who's responsible for this?" confusion.

- **Feedback loops**: Systems without feedback are static. Make iteration part of the rhythm. Build it in through weekly retros, scorecard reviews. and live dashboards.
- **Tech stack that scales with you**: Don't duct-tape your CRM to a spreadsheet and pray, audit your tools every quarter. Build infrastructure that doesn't buckle under growth.
- **Runbooks & playbooks**: Don't wait for chaos, pre-wire the response. When X breaks, here's how we fix it. That's operational maturity.

Here's a litmus test: if you disappeared for 30 days, would your team know exactly how to execute without calling you? If not, you don't have systems, you have dependency dressed up as hustle. Remember, I said great companies aren't built on hustle, they're built on architecture.

Retaining Top Talent – Keeping Your A-Players Engaged

There's a quiet tragedy playing out in most companies, and it's not the underperformers dragging things down. It's the A-players slowly checking out. Not because they hate the job, but because no one's keeping up with them. They're growing faster than the business, faster than the leadership, and when your best people start to feel unseen, underchallenged, or boxed in, you don't lose them overnight; you lose them in phases. We've established that first, their energy drops, then their initiative, then one day, they're gone, or they stay, but they've already quit inside.

The fact is, most leaders don't lose their top talent to competitors; they lose them to boredom.

Let's kill the myth now, pay isn't enough. Yes, people want to be compensated fairly, but once your best players hit a certain threshold, the currency that drives them shifts. They want growth, a challenge, and autonomy. They want to build, stretch, and contribute meaningfully, so if you don't give them that runway, someone else will or they'll go create it for themselves.

Ask any founder who scaled fast, they'll tell you: retaining your best people isn't just an HR goal, it's a survival strategy. In a high-growth company, your A-players are the compounding engine. They lift others, and they also build systems that can even take so much weight off your shoulders. Lose one and you don't just lose output, you lose leadership, momentum, and your culture carriers.

So you keep them by challenging them. Give them room to grow in the business, then reward them by partnering with them. Your A-players need stretch goals that make them sweat. They need big problems to solve, not busy work. Give them a mountain and watch them climb it. Give them a sandbox and they'll build a city, but if you give them a checklist and they'll give you their resignation.

They also need to see their future with you. Promotions aren't just about titles, they're about trajectory. If people don't know where they can go, they'll assume there's nowhere to go, so build visible growth paths and create internal ladders before your best people start looking for ones outside. Also, never forget this: top talent wants to be coached, not coddled. You don't have to handhold them, but you do have to invest in them. Regular feedback, stretch opportunities, and exposure to senior rooms; all aren't just luxuries, they're loyalty insurance.

I once worked with a fast-growing tech company where the CTO was a 10x engineer. Brilliant, obsessed, and dedicated guy, but he started pulling back because of boredom. The founder hadn't challenged him in months, so the work suddenly felt too easy, and the mission started to fade. By the time they tried to re-engage him, he'd already checked out. A year later, he was running engineering at a unicorn that gave him autonomy, ownership, and stretch. Lesson learned: don't just keep your stars busy, keep them burning.

Great leaders don't just keep talent, they amplify it. They put their best people in rooms that force growth. They delegate real ownership and say, "Here's a problem I don't know how to solve, own it." That's how loyalty is built. Not through comfort, but through trust.

So, ask yourself:

- Who on your team is ready for more right now but hasn't been given it?
- Who's stuck in a role they've outgrown?
- Who's so good at what they do that you've forgotten to challenge them?

Retaining talent involves purpose, so affirm their ownership, growth, and trust. Your A-players don't want to be entertained, they want to matter because when they do, they don't just stay, they soar. When they soar, so does everything you've built.

Hustler to Scaler

In a nutshell, there's an inevitable point in every leader's journey—provided your business is growing—when hustle is no longer enough. The long nights, the endless checklists, the doing-it-all-yourself mindset, it's what got you here. It's why your team follows you, and it's how you survived when things were fragile and new. But what gets you to survival will not get you to scale. Hustle might be the engine of early growth, but leadership is the engine of lasting transformation.

At some point, you stop being the center of everything, and you become the one who orchestrates everything. That means letting go of control to build capacity. It means releasing your grip on every decision so you can empower leaders who can decide without you.

Let me tell you about Carly. She was the business. She answered every phone call, closed every client, posted every social update, and handled every fire. She built something real through grit, care, and a refusal to let anything fall through the cracks. But as her company grew, the very habits that made her successful started to hold her back. She hired a team but never truly handed anything off. She clung to the "important stuff" because no one, in her eyes, could do it quite like she did. And maybe they couldn't at first, but instead of developing her team's confidence, she became their ceiling. When she stepped away for maternity leave, the business stumbled hard. Not because the idea was weak, not because the team lacked potential, but because everything was still running on her shoulders. Her company hadn't scaled, it had stretched, and trust me, stretched things eventually snap.

Through coaching, Carly began to understand that scaling wasn't about doing more. It was about leading differently. She shifted from Chief Execution Officer to Chief Validation Officer. Her new job wasn't to own every task, but to review, coach, and raise the bar. She started recording feedback videos. She gave her team space to grow, and she stopped expecting them to mirror her and started training them to think, act, and even innovate beyond her. Slowly, her mindset evolved. She didn't lower her standards, she raised her team. She didn't disappear, she changed how she showed up.

This is the shift every founder must make: from execution to elevation, from holding the weight to building the people who carry it, from "If I don't do it, it won't get done" to "If I teach it well, they'll do it better." Make no mistake, though, this transition isn't soft, it's brutal. It demands death to ego and also that you trust people before they've proven themselves. It asks you to let go of perfection so you can multiply progress. The very identity that made you successful now has to evolve, or it becomes your bottleneck.

To make that shift without losing momentum, you need more than just good intentions, you need structure. That's where proven delegation frameworks come in.

One of the most effective is the Eisenhower Matrix. It's built to help you decide what truly deserves your attention and what needs to be handed off or dropped altogether (Team Asana, 2025b). Picture four quadrants:

- Urgent & Important - Do it now.
- Important but Not Urgent - Schedule it.
- Urgent but Not Important - Delegate it.
- Not Urgent & Not Important - Eliminate it.

When you map your tasks like this, you stop reacting to every fire and start focusing on what drives real progress.

Another game-changer is the 70/20/10 Rule (Porumboiu, 2021). It's about how you allocate your leadership energy:

- 70% on core tasks - your bread and butter.
- 20% on growth - developing your team, building new systems.
- 10% on innovation - taking calculated risks that could elevate the whole operation.

Together, these frameworks keep you from becoming the bottleneck. They force you to hand off what's urgent but low-impact and spend your time on what truly moves the needle. That's how you scale without burning out.

That brings us to the honest question every founder has to face: Are you still building like a hustler, or are you scaling like a leader?

That shift is inevitable. The pain you feel right now—the stress, the chaos, the overwhelm—it isn't just a sign that you need to work harder, it's a sign that you need to lead differently. It's time to stop being the firefighter and start being the architect. Put down the toolbox and pick up the blueprint.

If you don't make the shift, growth will expose your cracks. It'll stretch your team thin, burn you out, and make you realize the hard way that hustle without systems is just a house of cards. However, if you embrace the shift, everything changes. You gain freedom, your team starts to flourish, your culture strengthens, and your company stops being an extension of you and becomes bigger than you.

That's the journey we just walked. We've covered how to transition from solo operator to systems builder, from being the glue to building a culture that sticks without you. We explored onboarding, delegation, developing leaders, scaling operations, and retaining the very people you once feared would never "get it." So, this isn't just a leadership checklist. It's a new operating system. One that demands more maturity, more intentionality, and a whole new identity as a leader. So, where do you begin?

Let's talk about what you can do first thing Monday morning.

MONDAY MORNING
PLAYBOOK

Scaling isn't about working harder, it's about leading smarter. Structure, delegation, and feedback loops. You're not building a hustle, you're building something that lasts.

🧠 MINDSET SHIFT:

If you're still gripping the wheel on every decision, you're the one slowing it down. Let go, or you'll crash at scale.

✓ DO THIS MONDAY:

1. Identify One Thing You're Still Doing That You Shouldn't Be (By End of Day Today)

- Be brutally honest: Is this a CEO/COO-level task, or am I just holding on to it?
  - Running reports? Scheduling meetings? Approving minor decisions?
- Choose one thing you know isn't your job anymore and delegate it this week.
- But don't just throw it over the fence, coach the handoff. Explain the why, not just the how.

2. Assess Your Leadership Layers (This Week)

- Open your org chart or list out your leadership structure.
  - Does anyone have more than 5–6 direct reports?
  - If yes, you're running a flat organization that's going to shatter under scale.
  - Decide where you need to build depth, create new layers, and promote new leaders.
- If you're the only decision-maker, you're not scaling, you're stalling.

3. Review One Process That's Still in Your Head (This Week)

- Pick one process you always "just do" without thinking.
  - It might be a client onboarding flow, a sales follow-up, or a reporting method.
- Document it. Teach it. Systematize it.
- If your brilliance is stuck in your head, you're the bottleneck. Get it out, train someone, and watch them run it.

CHAPTER 9:

PLAY TO WIN – THE HABITS, RHYTHMS, AND LEGACY OF A REAL LEADER

"What you leave behind is not what is engraved in stone monuments, but what is woven into the lives of others."

– Pericles

There's a powerful moment in *Black Panther* where T'Challa, freshly wounded and uncertain, finds himself face to face with his father in the ancestral plane. The old king looks his son dead in the eyes and delivers a truth that cuts deeper than any blade: "You're a good man, with a good heart, and it's hard for a good man to be king." That line wasn't just cinematic, it was spiritual. It wasn't questioning T'Challa's character; it was challenging his capacity because leadership involves more than just having good intentions or a strong vision. What does it require? An ability to carry the unbearable weight of responsibility while staying rooted in integrity. It's about making decisions that serve others even when they cost you personally. Most of all, it's about choosing growth, not just once, but repeatedly.

In many ways, every leader hits this same crossroads. At some point, you move past the survival phase; the fire-fighting, the hustle, the adrenaline highs, and you arrive at a quieter, heavier place. The systems are finally in place, the team is competent, and the chaos has settled into rhythm. However, in that calm, a new kind of question begins to whisper: "Am I still growing fast enough to deserve leading these people?" It's a confronting question because it flips the mirror. It forces you to evaluate your habits, your mindset, and your hunger, not based on what the business needs, but based on what your leadership is sowing into the people behind it.

The uncomfortable truth is that your team will rarely outperform the standard you set. They'll rise to your level or shrink beneath your inconsistency. While many leaders look outward for results, the best ones look inward for accountability. Your legacy won't be defined by your title, your revenue, or how many people reported to you. It will be defined by how you led when no one was clapping, how you grew when no one was watching, and how you treated people when you didn't need anything from them. It will be defined by whether or not your leadership multiplied leaders or just created dependencies.

Great leadership doesn't come from a conference, and it's certainly not found in a podcast highlight or a one-liner on LinkedIn. It's forged in the daily disciplines; the walks through the office where you stop to ask how someone's really doing, the moments you choose curiosity over control, and the silent commitment to keep raising your own bar even after everyone else thinks you've arrived. The day you stop growing is the day your team starts mentally clocking out. Not because the business outgrew you, but because you failed to grow with it. When you plateau, so does your

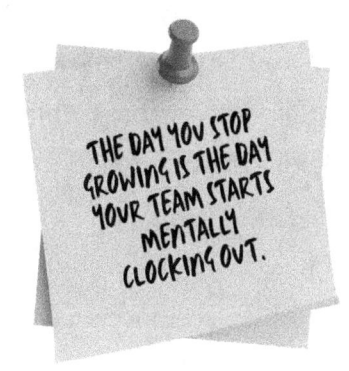

culture. What you built starts to decay not from outside forces, but from your own stagnation.

That's the unspoken obligation of leadership: don't just lead others—lead yourself. Not just to manage performance but to inspire transformation. Not just to build a company but to leave behind a culture that doesn't crumble the moment you step away. So, as we step into this final phase of the journey, the question shifts. It's no longer about what you can lead. It's about what you're willing to become in order to keep leading well. At the end of the day, leadership is not about reaching a throne; it's about building a foundation strong enough for others to stand on.

LEADERSHIP IS CAUGHT MORE THAN IT'S TAUGHT

The most transformative leadership lessons aren't absorbed in classrooms; they're caught in trenches, witnessed in moments, and forged in the crucible of real life. You can read a hundred books on communication, but people learn more from the way you speak to your team under pressure than from any slide deck. You can attend every leadership seminar on the planet, but if your actions don't reflect what you preach, your influence becomes hollow. Remember, people don't follow titles, they follow behavior, so they'll follow yours before they follow your instructions.

Some of the world's greatest leaders weren't molded in training programs, they were forged by circumstance. Think of Nelson Mandela. He didn't become a leader because someone handed him a guidebook on influence; he became one through the fire of injustice, the weight of responsibility, and the resolve to carry a vision bigger than himself (Nolen, 2013). Or consider Angela Merkel, who led with calm strength through the storms of economic crisis and refugee waves not because she was loud, but because she was steady. These weren't leaders shaped by theory alone; they were shaped by decision-making in real-time, in real stakes, when no manual could speak into the moment.

Even in business, we see it. Howard Schultz didn't learn servant leadership by reading about it, he learned it by watching his father struggle without dignity in the workforce. That pain became his compass. It shaped the way he built Starbucks around the dignity of every barista. These are leaders who didn't just talk about values but embodied them rather, even when no one was watching and that's the difference.

Let's be honest, how many people attend leadership conferences every year? Thousands. Maybe millions, but how many actual leaders are we producing? Leaders who can carry weight, not just repeat frameworks. Leaders who show up consistently, not just when the spotlight is on. The numbers don't lie, which tells us something critical: theory is helpful, but the school of life still produces the most unforgettable teachers. People don't become leaders because they learned the curriculum; they become leaders when the curriculum gets tested in crisis, and they choose integrity over ease.

That's why you can't outsource your development, because long before your team catches your strategy, they catch your spirit, your resilience, honesty, and humility. Leadership is contagious, but only if it's real. You are always teaching, even when you're unaware—especially when you're unaware. So, ask yourself: What is your team catching from you? What are they learning from the way you show up on a bad day? From the way you handle tension? From how you recover when you mess it up?

What you carry leaks, and whether it's fear or faith, scarcity or abundance, arrogance or empathy, that's what will spread.

So, if leadership is caught more than taught, the only way to build better leaders around you is to become one within yourself and that starts in the quiet places. The daily disciplines and the intentional habits that make up your unseen life because as you go, your team follows.

Let's get into the habits that anchor great leaders, especially when no one is looking.

Personal Mastery & Health Habits

Every great leader begins by leading themselves, and that starts with the body, the mind, and the daily rhythms that govern both. We've seen too many leaders crash, not from a lack of vision, but from a lack of vitality. You can't pour from an empty cup, especially when your role demands constant presence, decision-making, and emotional labor. That's why personal health isn't optional, it's foundational. Leaders who neglect their health end up borrowing energy from tomorrow to survive today, and eventually, the bill comes due.

Start with water. Yes—something as simple as hydration can dramatically affect your cognitive function, energy levels, and decision-making sharpness. The human brain is over 70% water, and studies show that even slight dehydration impairs short-term memory, mood, and focus (Zhang et al., 2019). Then comes sleep; Elon Musk is known for his grind, but even he's admitted that cutting sleep affected his performance. Leaders love to glorify late nights, but sleep is the original performance enhancer. Add to that a clean, consistent diet, regular movement (even just 30 minutes of walking), and strategic moments of rest and solitude.

Even Jesus, the greatest leader of all time, withdrew often, not because He was weak, but because He knew the power of restoration. Before feeding crowds or performing miracles, He'd retreat not as an escape plan, but to refuel. That's the rhythm: pour, refill, repeat. No one was busier than Him, yet He protected His peace. That's the standard.

Execution Habits

Once your inner world is disciplined, your outer execution starts to follow suit. The best leaders aren't just thinkers, they're builders; architects of vision and executors of plans. However, execution doesn't happen by accident, it's the byproduct of structure, prioritization, and an unwavering commitment to doing the right things—not just doing things right.

Great leaders don't confuse motion with progress. They know how to filter noise from a signal. They don't let a full inbox or a cluttered to-do list steal the spotlight from what really matters. That's why habits like setting daily priorities, reviewing your calendar with intention, and protecting deep work hours are nonnegotiable. It's not about being busy, it's about being effective.

Take leaders like Jeff Bezos, who famously says that his job is to make a few high-quality decisions each day. Not hundreds, not thousands, just a few decisions that really matter because if he gets those right, the rest falls into place. That's the principle: fewer things, done better, systems over stress, and focus over frenzy.

And remember, execution habits aren't just about doing the work; they're about sustaining the work. That means building in review rhythms such as weekly check-ins with yourself, monthly pulse checks with your team, and quarterly vision resets. You don't drift into excellence, you drive toward it with your habits as the wheel.

Relational Habits

Leadership involves establishing relationships, not just roles and responsibilities. The strength of your leadership is often measured by the quality of your connections. How you make people feel, how you build trust, and how consistently you show up for others, even when it's inconvenient.

Great leaders don't lead from a pedestal, they lead from proximity. They build rapport, not walls. They remember birthdays, check in when someone's off their game, and they listen without interrupting. These small acts, done consistently, form the glue that holds a culture together. Relational capital compounds, just like financial capital, but instead of interest, it pays in loyalty, resilience, and long-term buy-in.

Relational habits build psychological safety. When people feel seen and heard, they stop playing defense. They take risks, share ideas, and speak the hard truth. That's the foundation of every high-performing team: intentional connection that earns real trust.

One powerful practice is walking the floor regularly; not to micromanage, but to engage. Ask questions, offer encouragement, and give feedback in real time. Another one is holding consistent one-on-ones, not just to talk metrics, but to ask: "How are you really doing?", "What's frustrating you right now?", and "Where can I better support you?"

So, ultimately, strong leadership starts with strong relationships because people don't follow titles, they follow trust.

Spiritual/Legacy Habits

You can build the fastest company on earth, raise millions, hit every KPI, and still feel hollow as hell because when the purpose behind your grind gets blurry, the grind itself turns into a slow death. That's why the best leaders don't just stack goals, they anchor them. They build from within before they lead out loud. That's where spiritual and legacy habits come in.

Relax, we aren't talking about burning incense or chanting under waterfalls here. We are talking about staying grounded while the ground keeps shifting. Every high-level leader eventually realizes that if you don't make space to reconnect with your values, your mission, and the bigger picture, you'll get lost in the game you built. And worse, you'll lead other people off course too.

Take Phil Jackson; not just a basketball coach, but a full-blown philosopher in sneakers. The man had his team meditating before games, reading books on war strategy, and studying tribal leadership because he knew the battle wasn't just on the court, it was in the mind and in the spirit. Legacy isn't made in the scoreboard, it's made in the soul of the team, and that starts with a leader who's done the inner work.

Or think of Maya Angelou; not a CEO, but a titan of influence. She understood that how you show up internally affects everything you touch externally. Her daily practices, such as reflection, writing, and spiritual centering, weren't luxury rituals; they were survival and alignment tools (Clear, n.d.-b). She wasn't chasing titles, she was shaping legacy with every word, every silence, every stance.

So, what this means is that legacy is being written every damn day, whether you're aware of it or not. You don't need a statue or a farewell speech to build a legacy. It's in how you show up in the hard conversations. It's in how you talk to the intern when no one's watching. It's in how you bounce back after failure and whether you own the mess or spin it and be a coward who blames his subordinates.

Ask yourself: When your name comes up in a room full of people you once led, what tone will follow? Respect? Silence? A forced smile? That's your real scoreboard.

You can't fake your way into legacy; you've got to live it daily, intentionally, and spiritually because the higher you rise, the more your team feeds off your values, not your volume. They don't need a hype-man, they need a compass. So, before you think about building a monument to your success, build the habits that keep your soul in check. Remember, when the pressure's high, you will need your rhythms to keep you afloat.

Here's what that foundation looks like in the real world:

- **Daily Reflection** – Carve out 10 minutes to sit with your thoughts, your actions, and your motives. Not to judge, just to observe. Leaders who reflect lead with clarity, but the ones who don't just react.

- **Journaling for Alignment** – Not the "Dear Diary" type. I'm talking about jotting down values, tough moments, missteps, and course corrections. Think of it like a spiritual audit; raw, honest, and powerful.

- **Solitude & Silence** – Find a space where there's no noise. Not just physically, but mentally. This is where the best decisions are born.

- **Reconnecting with Purpose** – Read the mission. Rewrite it if you have to. Watch testimonials of others who've walked through fire and made it out. And don't get lazy or hide behind delegation; go to the frontline. Purpose is fuel, but only if you keep it fresh.

- **Legacy Visualization** – Ask yourself weekly: "If I keep leading like this, what will they say about me in 10 years?" If the answer sucks, it's time to shift.

- **Mentoring or Serving Beyond the Bottom Line** – Give back. Not for PR, but because greatness is never just about your rise, it's about who you lift along the way.

These aren't checkboxes, they're anchors. Practice them with consistency, and your leadership won't just spark inspiration, it'll stand the test of time.

Other Killer Habits Every Leader Should Build

- **Reading Daily (Even Just 10 Pages)**: Great leaders are obsessed with input; they know yesterday's wisdom won't win tomorrow's battles. Ten pages a day isn't much, but over a year, it's 3,650 pages of growth.

- **Asking Better Questions**: Leaders who ask sharp questions get sharper answers. "What do you need from me?" is a better question than "Is everything okay?" Good questions shift culture.

- **Listening Twice as Much as You Speak**: The best communicators aren't loud, they're curious. Listening is a form of leadership. It says: "You matter," and people who feel heard show up different.

- **Blocking Deep Work Time**: Leaders who stay reactive become burned out and ineffective. Deep work hours, no calls, no emails, just focused execution. This is where vision turns into progress.

- **Practicing Gratitude Daily**: Write three things down. Say thank you to your team, as a grateful leader isn't weak, they're grounded. And grounded leaders don't get knocked over by every storm.

- **Saying No Without Guilt**: Every "yes" is a "no" to something else. Protect your calendar like it's your life, because in leadership, it kind of is. You're not paid to please, you're paid to prioritize.

- **Making One Bold Move a Week:** Big vision requires action. Every week, push one thing forward that scares you. One hard conversation. One tough call. One major pitch. Momentum is built, not inherited.

Habits are what separate good leaders from great ones. That said, habits alone won't cut it. Sure, habits like walking the floor, showing up, and listening all keep the engine running, but great leaders don't just keep the boat afloat; they steer it toward something greater. They don't just delegate, they cultivate greatness, pushing their people to rise to new heights and that's the difference.

If you want to be a great leader, getting the job done isn't enough; you've got to pull others up with you. Inspire them to stretch, to grow, to go beyond what they thought was possible. Don't just manage people, develop them, challenge them, and show them there's more to chase than checklists and quotas. That's how real leadership leaves a mark.

HOLD THE MIRROR – STAY ACCOUNTABLE TO YOURSELF

I once worked with a founder whose name you wouldn't recognize, but her company is everywhere. Her team loved her, investors bet big on her, and she was hailed as one of the sharpest minds in her space. Visionary, fearless, efficient, and even on paper, she was a masterclass in leadership. But underneath the polish, something was slipping. Her energy was off, and her presence was thin. She stopped asking for feedback and also stopped listening to the people closest to the front lines. She was building her company at scale but shrinking herself in the process. Honestly, she didn't have a growth rhythm of her own, and without it, everything she had built started bending under pressure.

That's the quiet killer of leadership; you get so busy sharpening others, you forget to sharpen yourself. Even leaders like Indra Nooyi, former CEO of PepsiCo, speak often about the brutal pace and personal toll of leadership and how intentional rhythms of reflection and recalibration were her anchor. She didn't just show up to lead, she kept showing up to grow (McKinsey, 2021). Same goes for Whitney Wolfe Herd, founder of Bumble. At the height of her success, she took a step back to reevaluate her habits, her mental wellness, and what kind of leader she wanted to become next (Kirschner, 2023).

At a certain level, the difference between burnout and brilliance is whether you're still being coached or coasting.

Leadership is exhausting. Everyone wants a piece of you: your team, your investors, your clients, and even your family. So, amid the chaos, it's dangerously easy to stop growing. You're reading budgets instead of books, running meetings instead of running your own feedback loop, and you pour into others until you're dry. However, the moment you stop getting better, you start getting bitter. You get defensive then you stop listening. You fall back on past wins because present reality feels too confronting, and before long, you're leading on autopilot, just polished enough to survive, but not intentional enough to grow.

That's why the best leaders don't just coach, they get coached. They don't just expect accountability from others, they demand it from themselves because, without consistent inputs, your leadership becomes stale, predictable, repetitive, and eventually irrelevant.

So, how do the greats stay sharp? They build growth rhythms into their week, not just when things are quiet, but especially when things are chaotic.

Let's get practical:

1. Get in the room with people who are smarter than you. Every truly elite leader has a circle that challenges them. Not a fan club, not yes-men, but a real squad of thinkers who ask the hard questions and challenge the easy answers. That's why mastermind groups, coaching cohorts, and even dinner table conversations with other sharp leaders can be gold. Iron sharpens iron, so if you never feel friction, you're probably surrounded by foam.

2. Lock in weekly inputs. Podcasts, audiobooks, newsletters, long-form interviews, whatever stretches your perspective. Schedule it like a meeting and protect it like a client call. Growth doesn't happen by accident. Do you want to lead a company? Start by being a student of how others lead theirs. Consume material from completely different industries. Tech, fashion, sports, even nonprofits. Leadership principles are everywhere, you just have to notice the patterns.

3. Build feedback loops into your culture. We already discussed this, but just to briefly recap, if you're the only one talking, your blind spots are multiplying. The smartest

leaders create anonymous feedback channels, invite honest peer reviews, and normalize upward feedback. When it stings, they lean in because growth hurts before it helps. Try this: Once a month, ask someone on your team this brutal but brilliant question—"What's one way I'm making your job harder than it needs to be?" Then shut up. Listen. And fix it.

4. Retreat to recalibrate. Every high-output machine needs maintenance. You're no different. Schedule regular personal retreats not to check out, but to check in. Think, journal, reassess your vision. Ask: Am I leading from clarity or just reacting to the pressure? If Jesus withdrew to the mountains to pray, if CEOs lock in three-day offsites to strategize, what's your excuse? Even a single afternoon unplugged can give you perspective that a whole month of grinding can't.

5. Track your own growth like you track the team's. You've got KPIs for revenue, productivity, performance, but what about your personal growth? Create a leadership dashboard: What are you reading? Who's mentoring you? How are you handling stress? What hard thing have you gotten better at this quarter? The moment you take your own development as seriously as your team's, that's when real legacy leadership begins.

Accountability isn't a threat, it's protection. The higher you rise, the fewer people will check you, and that's the real danger. The most reckless leaders are the ones no one can challenge. If you want to stay sharp, stay humble, stay hungry, and keep people around you who'll tell you the truth, even when it stings.

MISTAKES MAKE YOU OR BREAK YOU

You will mess up, that's a guarantee. Whether it's misreading a situation, making a bad hire, greenlighting a strategy that flops, or letting your temper bleed into a conversation that needed grace, you will get it wrong at some point. However, leadership was never about perfection, it's about ownership and, more than that, it's about resilience. What separates the forgettable from the legendary isn't flawlessness; it's how they handle failure. Do they freeze, flinch, or blame others? Or do they step into the fire, take the hit, and come out of it sharper?

There's a dangerous illusion that starts to creep in as you rise through the ranks: that the higher up you are, the more you have to protect the image of being right. Well, the opposite is actually true; the higher you go, the more your response to being *wrong* defines your culture. People aren't watching for your perfection, they're watching for your posture. Your team takes its cue from how you recover. If you cover your tracks, so will they. If you deflect blame, they'll learn to do the same. But if you stand up, own it, and turn your mistake into a lesson, they'll trust you even more.

The most coachable leaders are the most durable because coachability is humility in motion. It's what keeps you from calcifying into your worst habits. It's what separates leaders who grow through the fire from those who get burned by it. If your pride is too loud to let anyone correct you, then you're already slipping, and your people probably already know it. Feedback is not a threat to your authority, it's the fuel that sustains it. You don't just coach others, you *get* coached. You seek it out, set the tone, and make it safe for people to tell you the truth, even when it stings.

In a high-performance culture, the goal is never to avoid mistakes but to turn every mistake into momentum. That means you build in rhythms of reflection. You debrief the losses just as much as you celebrate the wins. You ask the hard questions: What broke down? What did I miss? What should we never repeat again? Then you share those lessons. You normalize learning out loud because when your team sees you fall forward, they won't lose respect; they'll lean in. They'll realize this isn't a place where mistakes are fatal, but one where mistakes are fuel.

So, if you want to future-proof your leadership, don't obsess over the image of being bulletproof; build the muscle of being bounce-back strong. Get honest, get humble, and watch how you elevate.

Consider Sara Blakely, the founder of Spanx; before becoming the world's youngest self-made female billionaire, she was selling fax machines door-to-door and getting rejected daily. No background in fashion, no investors, just a relentless willingness to learn by doing and, often, failing. When Spanx first launched, she made blunders in packaging, marketing, and even pricing, but every misstep became a feedback loop. She'd adjust, refine, and improve. Blakely credits her father for asking her one question every day at dinner: "What did you fail at today?" In that household, failure wasn't shameful, it was celebrated as proof you were pushing the limits (Miller, 2021).

Or look at Reed Hastings, co-founder of Netflix; before the streaming giant disrupted the world, Hastings ran a company called Pure Software. It eventually sold for a decent amount, but he admitted he failed to build a strong, adaptable culture. Too much process and yet, not enough innovation. He micromanaged, and it stifled his team. That failure haunted him until he used it to build Netflix differently. In his own words: "Our culture of freedom and responsibility at Netflix was born out of the mistakes I made at Pure." He didn't bury his screw-ups. He used them as fertilizer for something better (Ian, 2025).

And then there's Whitney Wolfe Herd, founder of Bumble. Yes, we're talking about her again—she's that important here. After a very public departure from Tinder, marred by lawsuits and allegations of toxic leadership, she could've retreated. Instead, she took the hit and built something better. Herd didn't just recover, she redefined the industry. Bumble wasn't built in spite of her past experience, it was built because of it. She turned personal and professional failure into a platform for reinvention (Lotito, 2023).

These aren't polished success stories; they're messy, raw, and unfiltered, but they're also real, and that's what leadership looks like behind the scenes. Not the highlight reel or Instagram story, but the rebound. The fight to rise again when no one's watching. That's the thing about leadership. It's not forged in spotlight moments. It's formed in the quiet, painful, frustrating process of learning what *not* to do, and if you're not intentional about learning, you'll repeat the same mistakes in louder, costlier ways. Which leads us to something that ultimately defines what kind of leader you are…

LEGACY ISN'T WHAT YOU BUILD,
IT'S WHO YOU BUILD

If your name is the loudest thing you leave behind, you failed.

Let that sink in.

We've glamorized empire-building. We've gone over accountability, corner offices, billion-dollar valuations, and so on. But here's the cold truth: buildings crumble, products fade, and even your biggest wins get forgotten in the churn of progress. However, you know what doesn't? People you built who now build others—that's legacy. That's immortality.

Anyone can lead a team, but not everyone can build leaders. Want to know what real legacy looks like? It's when someone you mentored becomes a mentor themselves, and they don't even need to mention your name. The principles you instilled are so deeply embedded that your influence is felt without ever being seen. It's invisible leadership—the quiet echoes that outlive your applause.

Most leaders are obsessed with *scale* but the smartest ones obsess over *transfer*. You die with your potential but you live forever through your impact. Some of you are going to realize you've been building monuments to your ego, hiring people who stroke your genius, centralizing everything through you so you feel important. That's not leadership, that's insecurity in a power suit. And no one wants to inherit that.

If you want to build a legacy, stop managing and start multiplying. Empower others, share the mic, and let your team shine when you're not in the room, because if everything depends on you, that's poor leadership. Great leaders build systems and people that thrive without them. You're not the spotlight, you're the spark. Great leaders don't just produce outcomes, they produce people who can produce outcomes.

So, do you want to know how you'll be remembered? It won't be the posts you made, the targets you hit, or even the empire you built. People may forget the headlines, but they'll never forget how you made them feel. Legacy lives in people. In the ones who stood taller because you chose to bend low. In the ones who found their voice because you stepped back and handed them the mic. In the ones who kept running because you stayed behind just long enough to tie their shoes. You won't be remembered by the spotlight you stood in, but by the shadows you stepped out of so someone else could shine.

You're not just building a business, you're writing your eulogy—one decision, one leader, one investment at a time.

So, stop trying to be impressive and start being impactful. Legacy isn't about how high you went, it's about how many you took with you.

THE LEGACY OF ONE HONEST CONVERSATION

At one of my companies, I had a young team member—let's call him Bill. He was bright, driven, and overflowing with ideas and potential. But like many in their 20s, he had blind spots. Personal habits that weren't just slowing him down, but were silently setting him up to crash. However, I saw the spark, so I leaned in. Not with performance reviews or fancy frameworks but with brutal, honest, human conversation. The kind of talk that pierces ego and gets down to the marrow. I told him straight: "You're talented, but your habits are going to kill your future if you don't face them. Not just at work but in life generally."

I shared with him what one of my own mentors once told me:

"You've got more in you, but you've got to get out of your own way."

He listened, and honestly, it wasn't instant—it never is—but he did the work. Over the years, we kept in touch. Nothing fancy, just check-ins, encouragement, the occasional course correction, and then one day, he messaged me something I'll never forget:

"I'm just trying to be the kind of man you are."

He wasn't talking about my resume, he was talking about how I showed up, how I handled pressure, how I spoke truth, and how I lived.

Today, he's winning on every front. Married, leading, thriving, and I guarantee you, one day he'll have a Bill of his own to invest in.

That's legacy. Not a plaque, not a post, not a product, but a person. And that's the invitation for every leader reading this. You don't need a global stage to make a global impact, you just need the courage to build people.

So before you move on, wrestle with these:

Don't just highlight it and say "good point." Stop and sit with these because legacy isn't something you stumble into; it's something you design, one tough decision at a time.

Ask yourself:

- Who are three people in my life right now that I'm actively building—not managing, not directing—but *building*?

- If I disappeared today, what part of my leadership DNA would still live on in my team?
- Am I multiplying leaders or just building dependencies around me?
- When was the last time I told someone the truth that might have hurt in the short term but helped them long-term?
- Is my leadership style more about protecting my image or empowering others to rise?
- Am I building a culture that will outlast me or one that will collapse the moment I step back?
- What habits, phrases, and decisions of mine are unconsciously becoming the blueprint for others?
- Who poured into me that I need to honor by paying it forward?
- And here's the real one: "Would I want to be led by me?"

This isn't about knowing the right answers, it's about being brutally honest with yourself. Truth-telling is where the real work starts. If you can't hold yourself accountable, find someone who will. Someone who'll challenge you, push you, and refuse to let you coast.

Don't treat these questions as one-time reflections, let them stick. Reflect on them regularly, even daily. After all, building a legacy is a continual process.

So, as you wrestle with these truths and get real with yourself, the next step is action. Where do you go from here? How do you turn these reflections into real change in your day-to-day?

That's what the Monday Playbook is for. Let's take those hard truths and start building something real.

MONDAY MORNING
PLAYBOOK

Leadership isn't a finish line, it's a daily choice. Your team rises or falls to the level of your consistency. Legacy is what people remember when you're no longer in the room. If your leadership doesn't multiply, it dies with you.

🧠 MINDSET SHIFT:

You are both the ceiling and the floor, and your habits set the tone. Your mindset shapes the mood. If you want a better team, become a better leader. The standard you walk past is the standard you accept.

✓ DO THIS MONDAY:

1. Block 30 Minutes on Your Calendar This Week for Growth (Today)

- Pick one: A podcast, a book, peer coaching, or personal reflection. It doesn't matter what it is, just make it consistent.
- Leadership is a craft. If you're not sharpening it, you're dulling it.
- Book it now. If it's not on your calendar by the end of the day, you're pretending—not leading.

2. Ask Your Team for Feedback (This Week)

- Simple, clear, and vulnerable:
  - "What's one thing I could do differently to be a better leader for you?"
  - Listen. Don't justify or interrupt.
  - Thank them for their honesty, then actually use it. Your ego is not more important than their growth.

3. Revisit Your Legacy (Today)

- Ask yourself these three brutal questions:
  - "What will this team say about me when I'm gone?"
  - "Am I building something that lasts without me?"
  - "Am I modeling what I expect from them?"
- If the answers make you uncomfortable, good. That means you're still growing. Now lead differently.

CONCLUSION

A leader is best when people barely know he exists, when his work is done, his aim fulfilled, they will say: we did it ourselves.
–Lao Tzu

There's a moment in every leader's journey when they have to decide: Am I building something that just survives or something that *thrives*? Is this a team that just clocks in and coasts, or a team that shows up with fire, precision, and purpose? This whole book, then? It's a blueprint for the latter.

You don't get there by accident, and certainly not by filling seats with warm bodies or tolerating mediocrity because it's easier than confrontation. You get there by setting a standard so damn high, it scares away anyone who's not ready to bleed for it. You hire killers, not seat-fillers. You build culture through action, not slogans, and when someone's dragging the team down, you fire them fast, because nothing poisons a room quicker than tolerated incompetence.

It's not just who you bring in; it's who you turn them into. If you're not coaching, you're coasting. And if you're not holding people accountable, you're enabling mediocrity. So, do you want a team that actually gives a damn? Give a damn first, louder, harder, and more consistently than anyone else in the room.

You think the best teams you admire got there by accident? The ones that move with precision, execute with ruthless efficiency, and have each other's backs like it's life or death? That's culture, accountability, and—better yet—that's a leader who's not afraid to demand more.

And if you've made it through this book, if you've worked through the playbooks, then you already know what it takes. Monday morning is your battlefield, and your team is your weapon. Are you going to load it with blanks, or are you going to arm it to win?

Listen: *Kickass teams aren't born, they're built.* They're built through hiring the right people, holding the line when it matters, and cutting the dead weight before it poisons everything you've worked for. They're built by leading with precision, with standards that don't bend,  and with a mission that's bigger than just hitting targets.

The Final Challenge – Who's Suffering Because You Won't Lead?

So, let's not sugarcoat this; if your culture is slipping, your team is dragging, and mediocrity is setting up camp in the breakroom, it's on you. You can spin it however you want, but that's the truth.

Weak teams aren't the problem; weak leadership is. Culture rots from the top. If people are missing deadlines, phoning it in, or dragging their feet, it's because you allowed it. That's on your watch, and I don't care how many Monday morning pep talks you give or how many times you use the word "synergy" in your emails. If the standard is low, it's because you set it there.

So, here's the question you need to ask yourself, and not with that surface-level introspection cap. I mean *really ask yourself*, look-in-the-mirror-and-don't-blink kind of asking:

Who is suffering right now because you refuse to lead? Is it that high performer who's starting to check out because they're tired of carrying dead weight? Is it your team as a whole because you're tolerating B-player behavior to avoid conflict? Or maybe it's you burning out quietly because you won't make the hard calls?

You think you're being kind by giving second chances, by ignoring the warning signs, by avoiding those tough conversations, but let me be brutally clear: it's not kindness, it's cowardice. Every time you let mediocrity slide, you're lying to your team. You're telling them it's okay to coast. That average is acceptable. That good enough is good enough.

Unfortunately, mediocrity is contagious, and it spreads faster than excellence. It's the silent rot that creeps through your team, infecting even your best people until suddenly, your top performers start playing down to the level of the weakest link. I mean, why bust their ass when you're not willing to hold the line?

You want to know what leadership looks like? It's having the guts to call it out. To say, "This isn't good enough, and we're not accepting it." To tell the truth, even when it's uncomfortable, especially when it's uncomfortable.

So, here's your challenge:

1. Who do you need to lead better? Not "who needs to work harder." Who do you need to step up for? Who's floundering because you haven't been clear?

2. Where are you tolerating B-player behavior? You know exactly where it is. The person who skates by. The one who's always just good enough not to get called out. Cut that cancer before it spreads.

3. Where have you become the bottleneck? Yeah, I said it. *You.* Where are you slowing things down because you won't release control or make a decision?

If you're serious about building something that matters, you need to take a look in the mirror. You need to stop playing defense and start calling the damn plays. This is your team, your mission, your legacy, and right now, somebody's paying the price for your hesitation.

STOP PLAYING DEFENSE AND START CALLING THE DAMN PLAYS.

Legacy Lens – What Will They Say When You're Gone?

You want to know what your legacy really is? It's not the fancy title. It's not the corner office, the LinkedIn endorsements, or the plaques on the wall. It's what people say about you when you're not there to edit the script.

When you walk out that door for the last time, when the final Slack message is sent, and the office chair cools off, what's left? Do your people stumble in chaos? Or do they thrive because you built something that didn't need you hovering over it? That's the difference between real leadership and what I call "performative management." One's a torch that keeps burning, the other's a candle that flickers out the second you're gone.

Steve Jobs steps away from Apple, and it doesn't just survive; it becomes a juggernaut. Walt Disney passes on, and his empire doesn't collapse; it erupts into a global force. These weren't just leaders, they were architects of legacy; people who didn't just build companies, but carved movements into the world.

But then there's the other side. You know the type—the leader who leaves and the team collapses, processes fall apart, and deadlines get missed. The energy seeps out of the room like a slow bleed, and suddenly everyone's looking around, wondering what the hell happened. I'll tell you what happened: they didn't lead, they babysat. They micromanaged and hovered and clutched control so tightly that nobody else ever learned how to own the damn mission. They were the hero in their own story, but when the hero left, the kingdom burned.

So, here's the real question: When your team looks back, what are they going to say?

- Did you make them better?
- Did you force them to grow?
- Did you push them out of comfort and into capability?
- Or did you just keep things safe, keep things moving, and call it leadership?

If your people aren't stronger, sharper, and more dangerous than when they started, you failed. Leadership isn't maintenance, it's fortification. Build soldiers who don't just take orders but give them.

The way you lead now isn't just influencing your team's present, it's defining their future. Every time you reinforce the standard, you're pouring concrete. Every time you let it slip, you're cracking the foundation. Also, when your name is brought up in rooms you no longer enter, when people talk about you long after you're gone, what do they say? Do they say that you showed up and maintained or that you built something unbreakable?

Always remember that when the dust settles and the emails stop, you're not judged by what you did when you were there, you're judged by what still stands when you're not.

LEADING THROUGH, NOT AROUND

Back at PetSmart, the first time I stepped away, my team didn't just maintain, they evolved. They operated like I was still there, even when I wasn't. That cracked something open in me, but I didn't truly understand it until I led that next team.

This was different. I wasn't just stepping back, I was stepping through. I ran that PetSmart like a well-oiled warship, and not just once. We were ranked #1 in the entire country, year after year. This wasn't because I had my hands on every wheel or my eyes on every screen, but because I built leaders who didn't need me to move.

Each department was a fortress. We had specialists, people who didn't just wait for orders, but took real ownership. My leadership team wasn't just present, they were deeply invested. They held one-on-ones. They gave feedback without me prompting it, and they even celebrated wins and coached through the hard stuff, not because I demanded it, but because it was the culture.

Truth is, I felt useless and that discomfort hit hard. I was wired for trenches, not towers; used to making calls, fixing chaos but watching them thrive without me made it clear: they didn't need another soldier, they needed the architect.

They were doing cycle counts without my direction.

They were fixing problems I hadn't even seen yet.

They were leading, not because I told them to, but because that's who they had become.

That's when it hit me: The best teams aren't led by you, they're led through you.

When I finally stepped back, I didn't just see a team, I saw a machine. A living, breathing engine of ownership and accountability. I had stopped trying to do everything myself and instead became the validator. My job wasn't to fix, it was to fine-tune. Not to control, but to confirm. Hence, I didn't micromanage, I multiplied.

When you finally become the least needed, you become the most valuable. That's the legacy of real leadership: you don't build followers. You build leaders who build the next generation without you.

So, build the team and build the culture, or step aside for someone who will. Step back, look at what still stands without you… And there lies your legacy.

One Last Thing…

So really, I didn't write this manual just to add another book to your shelf. I wrote it because I've seen what happens when teams come alive, when cultures are built brick by brick, and when leaders stop babysitting and start building. I wrote it because I want you to experience what it's like to stand back, watch your team thrive without you, and realize you've just done the impossible; you made yourself unnecessary.

That's the real win. That's the legacy.

So, here's to you building something that lasts, leading like it matters, and never settling for anything less than kickass. I appreciate you taking this journey with me, and I can't wait to see what you build next.

If you've made it this far, you know what it takes to build a team that actually gives a damn. But that's just the beginning. The real challenge? Well, the next frontier is running the entire business with that same level of clarity, alignment, and relentless execution. That's exactly what my next book, *The Rule of 3*, is all about. Consider this your blueprint for building warriors. The next step is leading them across the battlefield.

But before you go charging out to make your mark, let's do one final gut check. If you're serious about building something that lasts, you can't leave it to chance.

Here's your *Kickass Team Checklist*:

This is the last filter, the final playbook to make sure you're not just talking leadership, you're living it. If you can't confidently check these off, you're not ready to scale, you're still playing defense, and that's not what we came here to do.

Kickass Team Checklist

Check yourself before you wreck your culture. These ideas are here to become your standards.

Leadership & Ownership:

- I show up every day with intention and consistency.
- I hold myself accountable before I hold anyone else accountable.
- I give honest, direct feedback, especially when it's uncomfortable.

Hiring & Culture Fit:

- Every person on my team aligns with our core values.
- I don't hire out of desperation. I don't hire out of convenience.
- I've built a bench of potential future hires and promotions.

Expectations & Accountability:

- Every role has clear expectations and a current scorecard.
- My team knows exactly what success looks like.
- Underperformance isn't swept under the rug, it's addressed immediately.

Coaching & Communication:

- I hold weekly 1-on-1s with each direct report, no exceptions.
- I know what motivates each person on my team.
- Feedback is timely, specific, and constructive.

Culture & Momentum:

- We celebrate wins and reinforce values consistently, not just when it's convenient.
- Our communication cadence is strong, predictable, and transparent.
- Team members feel safe to speak up and take risks without fear of judgment.

Scalability & Structure:

- I've delegated key responsibilities and trust my team to deliver.
- No leader on my team has more than 5-6 direct reports.
- Systems are in place to support growth without burning people out.

If you can't confidently check off at least 80% of this list, you don't have a team problem, you have a leadership opportunity. And that's on you to fix.

So, my friends, I'm not asking you to be perfect, I'm asking you to raise the standard.

Leadership is a craft. Master it and you don't just build a team, you build a legacy.

Oh, and let me leave you with just one final thought to ponder:

If your entire team were interviewed tomorrow and had to describe your leadership in one sentence, would you be proud of what they'd say?

REFERENCES

Amazing Workplaces. (2023, September 9). *Gore-tex: Leading clothing retailer with a unique work culture*. Amazing Workplaces. https://amazingworkplaces.co/gore-tex-where-integrity-teamwork-and-innovation-unite/

American Psychological Association. (2023, November 15). *APA dictionary of psychology*. APA. org; American Psychological Association. https://dictionary.apa.org/culture

Anderson, D. (2014, September 16). *Building team culture: Marinate your people - Dave Anderson*. Anderson Leadership Solutions. https://www.andersonleadershipsolutions.com/to-build-a-low-maintenance-team-culture-marinate-your-people/

Angelou, M. (n.d.). *Your legacy is every life you've touched*. Threads. Retrieved May 12, 2025, from https://www.threads.com/@readswithravi/post/DH7dXpEtMXj/5-your-legacy-is-every-life-youve-ever-touched-maya-angelou

Archives, U. N. (2023, June 9). *"Outstanding veterans": Major Dick Winters*. The Reagan Library Education Blog. https://reagan.blogs.archives.gov/2023/06/09/outstanding-veterans-major-dick-winters/

Arets, J., Jennings, C., & Heijnen, V. (n.d.). *The 70:20:10 Model - A different view of work, performance and learning*. 70:20:10 Institute. https://702010institute.com/702010-model/

Bannister, B. (2024, March 21). *Leadership Lessons from Howard Schultz the manager who built Starbucks*. IManage Performance. https://imageperformance.com/blog/leadership-lessons-from-howard-schultz-the-manager-who-built-starbucks/

Benton, L. (2022, March 15). *Zappos - The culture everyone wants to copy*. Liberty Mind. https://libertymind.co.uk/zappos-the-culture-everyone-wants-to-copy/

Blanchard, K. (n.d.). *In the past a leader was a boss. Today's leaders must be partners with their people... they no longer can lead solely based on positional power.* Asana. https://asana.com/resources/business-quotes

Bondarenko, P. (2025a). Enron Scandal. In *Encyclopædia Britannica*. https://www.britannica.com/event/Enron-scandal

Bondarenko, P. (2025b). Enron scandal. In *Encyclopædia Britannica*. https://www.britannica.com/event/Enron-scandal

Buonarroti, M. (n.d.). *The greatest danger for most of us is not that our aim is too high and we miss it, but that it is too low and we reach it.* Goodreads. https://www.goodreads.com/quotes/557979-the-greatest-danger-for-most-of-us-is-not-that

Cancialosi, C. (2017, May 30). *Preserving a culture people love as your company grows: Lessons from Zappos.* Forbes. https://www.forbes.com/sites/chriscancialosi/2017/05/30/preserving-a-culture-people-love-as-your-company-grows-lessons-from-zappos/

Center for Creative Leadership. (2022, November 18). *Use SBI (situation-behavior-impact) to understand intent | CCL.* CCL. https://www.ccl.org/articles/leading-effectively-articles/closing-the-gap-between-intent-vs-impact-sbii/

Clear, J. (n.d.-a). *"You do not rise to the level of your goals. You fall to the level of your systems."* James Clear. https://jamesclear.com/quotes/you-do-not-rise-to-the-level-of-your-goals-you-fall-to-the-level-of-your-systems

Clear, J. (n.d.-b). *Masters of habit: The wisdom and writing of Maya Angelou.* James Clear. https://jamesclear.com/maya-angelou

Clifford, C. (2018, May 29). *Former Apple CEO John Sculley: What I learned from Steve Jobs.* CNBC. https://www.cnbc.com/2018/05/29/what-ex-apple-pepsi-ceo-john-sculley-learned-from-steve-jobs.html

Clover HR. (n.d.). *How NVIDIA's organisational culture drives its success.* Clover HR. https://www.cloverhr.co.uk/blog/nvidia-organisational-culture/

Collier, J. (2025, February 6). *Jimmy Butler timeline - Dysfunction, stormy practices and six All-Star Games - ESPN.* ESPN; ESPN. https://www.espn.ph/nba/story/_/id/43587920/jimmy-butler-line-dysfunction-infamous-practices-six-all-star-games

Cote, C. (2023, September 7). *5 strategies for conflict resolution in the workplace.* Harvard Business School Online; Harvard Business School Online. https://online.hbs.edu/blog/post/strategies-for-conflict-resolution-in-the-workplace

Cranmer, F. (2017, March 20). *The Bishop of the River of Hippopotamuses and the Archbishop of Cape Town | Law & Religion UK.* Lawandreligionuk.com. https://lawandreligionuk.com/2017/03/20/the-bishop-of-the-river-of-hippopotamuses-and-the-archbishop-of-cape-town/

CX recovery tactics: Ritz-Carlton's $2K empowerment rule and its impact. (2025). FML. https://freemarketingleads.co/home/2025/03/07/cx-recovery-tactics-ritz-carltons-2k-empowerment-rule-and-its-impact-on-luxury-hospitality/

Dick Winters' first battle. (2022). Beaches of Normandy Tours. https://www.beachesofnormandy.com/articles/Dick_Winters_first_battle/?id=39de8c64c0&utm

Dimopoulos, S. (2016, June 18). *W.L. Gore: Lessons from a management revolutionary.* Linkedin. https://www.linkedin.com/pulse/wl-gore-lessons-from-management-revolutionary-spiros-dimopoulos

EQS Editorial Team. (2023, November 22). *Elizabeth Holmes and the Theranos Case: History of a fraud scandal.* EQS Integrity Line. https://www.integrityline.com/expertise/blog/elizabeth-holmes-theranos/

Feldman, A. (2019, November 18). Here's what happened to WeWork's other founder, Miguel McKelvey. *Forbes.* https://www.forbes.com/sites/amyfeldman/2019/11/18/heres-what-happened-to-weworks-other-founder-miguel-mckelvey/

Geraghty, T. (2022, September 30). *Psychological safety: The Andon Cord.* Psych Safety. https://psychsafety.com/psychological-safety-79-the-andon-cord/

Goldsmith, M. (n.d.). *What got you here won't get you there.* Marshall Goldsmith. https://marshallgoldsmith.com/book-page-what-got-you-here/

Gottlleb, E. (2023, April 23). *The 10 commandments of feedback: Commandments 3-5.* Psychology Today. https://www.psychologytoday.com/za/blog/the-evolving-self/202409/the-10-commandments-of-feedback-commandments-3-5

Greenhalgh, N. (2023, June 13). *Leadership vs. management: The key differences.* Daniels College of Business; University of Denver. https://daniels.du.edu/blog/leadership-vs-management/

Helmore, E. (2023, November 7). The dizzying rise, and even more vertiginous fall, of WeWork. *The Guardian.* https://www.theguardian.com/business/2023/nov/06/wework-bankruptcy-rise-fall

Iacocca, L. (n.d.). *I hire people brighter than me and then I get out of their way.* Testlify. https://testlify.com/insightful-quotes-about-hiring/

Ian. (2025, March 4). *5 failures of Netflix CEO Reed Hastings & how he overcame them.* Pressfarm. https://press.farm/5-failures-netflix-ceo-reed-hastings-overcame/

The Investopedia Team. (2021, July 19). *Gamification definition.* Investopedia. https://www.investopedia.com/terms/g/gamification.asp

James, L. (2023, January 22). *How Nelson Mandela's former prison guard is keeping his legacy alive.* The Independent. https://www.independent.co.uk/news/world/africa/nelson-mandela-christo-brand-prison-apartheid-b2265675.html

Kirschner, K. (2023, November 19). *Bumble founder Whitney Wolfe Herd's daily routine starts at 5:15 a.m.* Business Insider. https://www.businessinsider.com/bumble-founder-whitney-wolfe-herd-daily-routine-work-schedule-2023-11

Lair, P. (2016, April 24). *Impulsive vs. Decisive.* The Bohol Chronicle. https://www.boholchronicle.com.ph/2016/04/24/impulsive-vs-decisive/

Laoyan, S. (2025, January 21). *Overcome analysis paralysis with these 4 tips.* Asana. https://asana.com/resources/analysis-paralysis

Lipcamon, J. (2016, October 31). *Ten commandments of feedback.* Diagnostic Imaging. https://www.diagnosticimaging.com/view/ten-commandments-feedback

Lotito, J. (2023, November 21). *What we can learn from Whitney Wolfe Herd's Bumble transition.* Forbes. https://www.forbes.com/sites/jenniferlotito/2023/11/21/what-we-can-learn-from-whitney-wolfe-herds-bumble-transition/

Lyons, D. (2019, October 4). *The real victims of WeWork are its employees. Is capitalism broken? - from day one.* Fromdayone. https://www.fromdayone.co/2019/10/04/the-real-victims-of-wework-its-employees-is-capitalism-broken/

MacNeil, C. (2025, April 11). *30-60-90 day plan: How to onboard new hires with ease.* Asana. https://asana.com/resources/30-60-90-day-plan

Major Richard Winters. (n.d.). Band of Brothers Wiki. https://wikiofbrothers.fandom.com/wiki/Major_Richard_Winters

Malone, M. R. (2021, September 15). *Theranos trial highlights the dark side of leadership.* News.miami.edu. https://news.miami.edu/stories/2021/09/theranos-trial-highlights-the-dark-side-of-leadership.html

Mark, M. (2013, December 11). *Mandela's jail warden tells how a man he saw as a terrorist became a "brother."* The Guardian; The Guardian. https://www.theguardian.com/world/2013/dec/11/mandela-jail-warden-terrorist-brother-jack-swart

McCord, P. (2014, February). *How Netflix reinvented HR.* Harvard Business Review; Harvard Business Review. https://hbr.org/2014/01/how-netflix-reinvented-hr

McGroarty, K. (2022, January 24). *Common leadership conflicts in the workplace.* Pollack Peacebuilding Systems. https://pollackpeacebuilding.com/blog/common-leadership-conflicts-in-the-workplace/

Mckinsey. (2021, October 8). *Author talks: Indra Nooyi on leadership, life, and crafting a better future | McKinsey.* McKinsey & Company. https://www.mckinsey.com/featured-insights/mckinsey-on-books/author-talks-indra-nooyi-on-leadership-life-and-crafting-a-better-future

Miller, H. (2021, November 18). *Sara Blakely: 7 lessons from a self-made billionaire.* Leaders. https://leaders.com/articles/women-in-business/sara-blakely-spanx/

Morrison, D. (n.d.). *The standard you walk past is the standard you accept*. Www.ft.lk. Retrieved May 6, 2025, from https://www.ft.lk/columns/The-standard-you-walk-past-is-the-standard-you-accept/4-747662

Morse, E. R. (2020). *The origins of Ritz-Carlton's famous $2,000 rule - the work of Eric Robert Morse*. Eric Robert Morse. https://ericrobertmorse.com/the-origins-of-ritz-carltons-famous-2000-rule/?utm

Murillo, K. R. (2017, March 15). *What you allow, will continue. – Katherine Rose*. Onairwithkat.com. http://onairwithkat.com/what-you-allow-will-continue/

Muse. (2023, April 7). *Spotlight: Phil Jackson - mindfulness in basketball*. Choosemuse. https://choosemuse.com/blogs/news/spotlight-phil-jackson-mindfulness-in-basketball

Nader, R. (n.d.). *The function of leadership is to produce more leaders, not more followers. - Ralph Nader*. Dr. Gary Fox. https://www.garyfox.co/quote/function-leadership/

Netflix. (2024). *Netflix culture — The best work of our lives*. Netflix. https://jobs.netflix.com/culture

Nolen, S. (2013, December 5). Mandela's miraculous capacity for forgiveness a carefully calibrated strategy. *The Globe and Mail*. https://www.theglobeandmail.com/news/world/nelson-mandela/mandelas-miraculous-capacity-for-forgiveness-a-carefully-calibrated-strategy/article548192/

Olivier, J. (n.d.). *The meaning of radical candor: What it is and how to use it*. Teammaven.io. https://www.teammaven.io/blog/the-meaning-of-radical-candor-what-it-is-and-how-to-use-it

Pacelli, L. (2021, March 15). *"Get it done yesterday!" Impulsive vs. Deliberate leadership decision making*. Linkedin. https://www.linkedin.com/pulse/get-done-yesterday-impulsive-vs-deliberate-leadership-lonnie-pacelli/

Petrikowski, N. P. (2025). Angela Merkel | Biography, political career, & facts. In *Encyclopædia Britannica*. https://www.britannica.com/biography/Angela-Merkel

Pollack, J. (n.d.). *3 types of workplace conflict & how to resolve them effectively | allwin conflict resolution training*. AllWin Conflict Resolution Training. https://conflict-resolution-training.com/blog/types-of-workplace-conflict/

Pollack, J. (2024, September 7). *What is relationship conflict? Definition, examples & resolutions*. Pollack Peacebuilding Systems. https://pollackpeacebuilding.com/blog/relationship-conflict/

PON Staff. (2022, October 17). *Value conflict: What it is and how to resolve it*. PON - Program on Negotiation at Harvard Law School. https://www.pon.harvard.edu/daily/conflict-resolution/resolving-conflicts-deeply-held-values-nb/

Porumboiu, D. (2021, August 27). *What is the 70-20-10 rule of innovation and how to use It.* Viima. https://www.viima.com/blog/70-20-10-rule-of-innovation

Radical Candor Framework. (n.d.). Modelthinkers. Retrieved May 3, 2025, from https://modelthinkers.com/mental-model/radical-candor-framework

Reagan, R. (n.d.). *Peace is not the absence of conflict, but the ability to handle conflict by peaceful means.* BrainyQuote. https://www.brainyquote.com/quotes/ronald_reagan_169550

Robinson, C. (2025, April 21). *How decision fatigue quietly sabotages leadership and what to do.* Forbes. https://www.forbes.com/sites/cherylrobinson/2025/04/21/how-decision-fatigue-quietly-sabotages-leadership-and-what-to-do/

Rose, V. (2020, April 17). *Value conflict: Definition, examples, and resolutions.* Pollack Peace Building. https://pollackpeacebuilding.com/blog/value-conflict/

Rosenthal, T. (2022, May 11). *Indra Nooyi is purpose and power personified.* Columbia Business School. https://business.columbia.edu/leadership-and-ethics-news/bernstein-center-leadership-and-ethics/indra-nooyi-purpose-and-power

Showdown at Apple: John Sculley vs. Steve Jobs - Mac History. (2008, October 30). MAC-HISTORY-NET. https://www.mac-history.net/showdown-at-apple-john-sculley-vs-steve-jobs/

Talent Management Institute. (n.d.). *The complete guide to creating effective 30-60-90 day plans for new employees.* Talent Management Institute. https://www.tmi.org/blogs/the-complete-guide-to-creating-effective-30-60-90-day-plans-for-new-employees

Team Asana. (2025a, January 29). *The Eisenhower matrix: How to prioritize your to-do list.* Asana. https://asana.com/resources/eisenhower-matrix

Team Asana. (2025b, January 29). *The Eisenhower matrix: How to prioritize your to-do list.* Asana. https://asana.com/resources/eisenhower-matrix

10 strategies to sharpen your decision-making skills as a leader. (n.d.). Hagbergconsulting. https://www.hagbergconsulting.com/10-strategies-to-sharpen-your-decision-making-skills-as-a-leader

Tenney, M. (2022). *The best company culture in the world.* PeopleThriver. https://peoplethriver.com/what-is-the-best-company-culture/

Toporek, A. (2022, September 27). *The Ritz-Carlton's famous $2,000 rule.* Customers That Stick. https://customersthatstick.com/blog/the-ritz-carltons-famous-2000-rule/

Toyota cutting the fabled andon cord, symbol of Toyota Way | Lean Manufacturing Times. (2014, August 19). Lean Manufacturing Times. https://www.leanmanufacturingtimes.com/toyota-cutting-fabled-andon-cord-symbol-toyota-way/

Tzu, L. (n.d.). *A leader is best when people barely know he exists, when his work is done, his aim fulfilled, they will say: we did it ourselves.'*. BrainyQuote; BrainyQuote. https://www.brainyquote.com/quotes/lao_tzu_121709

Valenzuela, A. (2023, November 21). *Elements of culture: Explanation of the major elements that define culture video with lesson transcript.* Study.com. https://study.com/academy/lesson/elements-of-culture-definitions-and-ideal-real-culture.html

Wheeler, W. L., & Wheeler, K. (2022, November 28). *Leading by example: The Socratic method of teaching and servant leadership.* Electrical Contractor; Electrical Contractor Magazine. https://www.ecmag.com/magazine/articles/article-detail/leading-by-example-the-socratic-method-of-teaching-and-servant-leadership

Williams, S. (n.d.). *7 legendary leadership lessons from Phil Jackson's coaching career.* Insider. catalystleader.com. https://insider.catalystleader.com/read/7-legendary-leadership-lessons-from-phil-jacksons-coaching-career

Willink, J. (n.d.-a). *Discipline equals freedom.* Goodreads. https://www.goodreads.com/work/quotes/55537924-discipline-equals-freedom-field-manual

Willink, J. (n.d.-b). *When it comes to standards, as a leader, it's not what you preach, it's what you tolerate. When setting expectations, no matter what has been said or written, if substandard performance is accepted and no one is held accountable.* Goodreads. Retrieved May 8, 2025, from https://www.goodreads.com/quotes/8595328-when-it-comes-to-standards-as-a-leader-it-s-not?

Yoda. (n.d.). *Do or do not, there is no try.* Goodreads. Retrieved May 13, 2025, from https://www.goodreads.com/author/quotes/13493815.Yoda

Zaleznik, A. (2004, January). *Managers and leaders: Are they different?* Harvard Business Review. https://hbr.org/2004/01/managers-and-leaders-are-they-different

Zhang, N., Du, S. M., Zhang, J. F., & Ma, G. S. (2019). Effects of dehydration and rehydration on cognitive performance and Mood among Male College Students in Cangzhou, China: A Self-Controlled Trial. *International Journal of Environmental Research and Public Health, 16*(11), 1891. https://doi.org/10.3390/ijerph16111891

www.ingramcontent.com/pod-product-compliance
Lightning Source LLC
Chambersburg PA
CBHW062319120626
46546CB00013B/1892